LEARNING MACHINE LEARNING VIA MEMORABLE STORIES

Designed & Crafted by

Oguzhan Topsakal

FOREWORD

THE power of stories is timeless. We, as humans, have an innate connection to narratives, finding them instantly memorable and engaging. Allow me to share a personal narrative:

During my elementary years, I often found myself lost in daydreams during class, my attention wandering, unable to remain anchored to my teacher's words. However, the moment he would begin weaving tales from his personal journey, my mind would snap to attention, hanging onto every word.

This challenge persisted as I moved through middle school, where lectures on mathematics or science would quickly become a blur, while those on history or religion, rich in stories, would captivate me. Observing my peers seemed effortlessly absorbing lectures, I felt embarrassed, keeping my struggle a secret. This trend shadowed me through high school, university, and even into graduate studies. Yet, in spite of this, I became adept at last-minute studies, always managing to excel in exams.

A few years back, while attending a presentation by an angel investor, a particular insight struck me. Recounting a day of listening to pitches from over 50 startup founders, he posed a question: "Of all the products presented, which ones lingered in my memory?" He revealed that it was those products intertwined with a compelling narrative.

This revelation, combined with my personal experiences, ignited the inspiration behind this book.

This book offers a unique journey into machine learning, told through memorable stories. Each concept in this book is explored through three different stories, and each story is packed with clever analogies to help you understand better. After the stories, we present each concept at three tiers of depth: simplified, general, and detailed, allowing readers to progressively deepen their understanding. These engaging narratives and clear explanations are crafted by OpenAI's ChatGPT, a cutting-edge AI large language model renowned for its proficiency. To enhance each story further, striking visuals are created by another AI wonder from OpenAI, known as Dall-E.

I wish to extend my deepest gratitude to all researchers and engineers in the field of AI, with a special nod to the team at OpenAI. Their pioneering work, especially in developing remarkable products like ChatGPT, laid the foundation for this book. Without their ingenuity and hard work, this endeavor would not be possible.

As we stand on the precipice of an AI-driven era, I hope this resource will offer valuable insights and clarity to newcomers, non-technical readers, and all who venture into the realm of machine learning.

Sincerely,

Oguzhan Topsakal, Ph.D.

PREFACE

IN the evolving tapestry of technology, machine learning stands out as one of the most captivating threads. Its essence lies not just in algorithms or vast datasets, but in the transformational power it wields, reshaping industries and redefining the boundaries of what machines can achieve. Yet, for many, the domain remains obscured by jargon, complexity, and a sense of the abstract.

With "Learning Machine Learning via Memorable Stories", we embark on a unique journey to unveil the magic of machine learning, not through intimidating equations or technical lingo, but through the universal language of stories. Every civilization, every culture, and every heart connects to stories; they are the timeless vessels of knowledge, values, and insights.

These tales, born from a collaboration between a visionary editor/designer and the linguistic marvel known as ChatGPT, are artfully interwoven with analogies. As you traverse this narrative landscape, you'll not only understand the foundational concepts of machine learning but also feel the wonder, challenges, and aspirations that drive this field.

Furthermore, following the stories, we explain each concept at three distinct levels of depth: simplified, general, and detailed, leading readers to a progressively profound comprehension.

This book is for the curious minds, whether you're a student just beginning to wonder about the world of artificial intelligence, a professional keen to unravel its impact on your industry, or simply someone who loves a good story. In these pages, we aim to bridge the gap between the technical and the mystical, making machine learning not just a subject to be studied, but an adventure to be experienced.

We invite you on this journey to explore, dream, and discover. Welcome to this unique book, where tales of magic and machine intertwine.

Warmly,

ChatGPT

This preface was generated using a prompt.

WHO THIS BOOK IS FOR

THIS book is a valuable resource for a wide audience. It is a great fit for non-technical individuals who have a curiosity about machine learning and want to deepen their understanding. Additionally, professionals with a technical background outside of computer science can also greatly benefit from the approachable and insightful content presented in this book. Moreover, high school or even middle school students and teachers seeking an engaging and introductory experience with machine learning concepts will find it to be a delightful start.

CONTENTS

CHAPTER 1

WHAT IS MACHINE LEARNING

In the next section, we delve into three illustrative tales that demystify both 'What is machine learning?' and 'How does it operate?'. Following each story, we unravel the metaphors to give you a clearer understanding. Subsequently, we provide explanations at three levels of complexity simplified, general, and detailed; allowing for a progressive deepening of understanding.

1.1 STORY: "THE MAGIC COOKBOOK"

Once upon a time, in a town named Predictville, there was a magical cookbook named "Learno." Learno wasn't like any regular cookbook. Instead of having a fixed list of recipes from the start, its pages were blank.

A young chef named Maya inherited Learno. The first time she tried to use it, she was puzzled. "How can I cook with an empty cookbook?" she wondered. But the magic of Learno was special. Maya would cook a dish, write down the ingredients and steps in Learno, and rate how tasty the dish was.

Figure 1.1: Prompt: a picture of a chef cooking next to a magical book

Each time Maya cooked and recorded her results, Learno would recommend slight changes to improve the dish. "Add a bit more salt," it would suggest, or "Cook for five minutes less." The more dishes Maya made, the better Learno's suggestions became.

Over time, Maya realized that Learno was learning from every dish she made. She didn't need to tell it how to make a perfect dish; it figured it out based on the feedback from each recipe attempt. Eventually, with Learno's help, Maya became the most renowned chef in Predictville.

ANALOGY EXPLANATION

- *Learno (the magic cookbook)* represents a *machine learning model*. Just like Learno started with blank pages, a machine learning model often starts without knowledge.

- *Maya* represents a *data scientist or developer* who trains the machine learning model.

- The *process of cooking different dishes* and recording outcomes represents the *training data and training process* in machine learning. Every dish Maya makes and records is like inputting a new data point into the model.

- The *ratings Maya gave* for how tasty each dish was are analogous to *feedback or labels* in supervised learning. This feedback helps the model understand how well it's doing and what it needs to adjust.

- The *suggestions from Learno* represent the *predictions or recommendations* a machine learning model would provide after being trained on enough data.

- Over time, as more recipes (data points) are added and feedback (labels) is given, Learno (the model) gets better and better at giving recommendations, just like a machine learning model improves its accuracy with more training data.

In essence, machine learning is like the magical cookbook: it learns patterns from provided data and, based on that, makes predictions or decisions, improving its accuracy over time with more data and feedback.

1.2 STORY: "LENNY, THE ROCK SCULPTOR"

IN a small village, there was a young boy named Lenny who loved sculpting rocks. One day, his grandmother gave him a challenging task. She showed him a collection of rocks and said,

"Lenny, I want you to create the most beautiful bird sculptures from these rocks."

Excited, Lenny picked up the first rock and began chiseling. However, it turned out pretty rough. Determined, Lenny decided to pay attention to the errors he made and started sculpting the next rock with a few tweaks based on his previous mistakes. With each rock he sculpted, Lenny made fewer mistakes and improved his technique, learning from each previous attempt.

Eventually, the village gathered in amazement, observing that Lenny's latest sculptures were much more refined and lifelike than the initial ones. By practicing and learning from his mistakes, Lenny had mastered the art of sculpting birds.

ANALOGY EXPLANATION

- *Lenny* represents a *machine learning algorithm*. Just as Lenny started with little knowledge about sculpting birds and improved over time, an algorithm starts with random predictions and refines them based on feedback.

- The *collection of rocks* can be likened to *data points* in machine learning. Each rock Lenny sculpted is like an instance the algorithm trains on.

- The act of *sculpting* represents the *training process*. Just as Lenny adjusted his technique with each rock, the algorithm updates its predictions with each piece of data.

- Lenny's *improvement* in his sculptures over time is analogous to the *iterative learning* process in machine learning. With each rock (data point) and every mistake (error in prediction), Lenny (the algorithm) learns and becomes better.

- The *villagers' amazement* at the end is similar to the end goal of machine learning: achieving a high level of *accuracy or precision* in predictions after sufficient training.

In essence, just as Lenny learned and perfected his craft of sculpting birds from rocks by iterating and learning from

Figure 1.2: Prompt: A young boy chiseling rocks into bird sculptures, evolving in detail.

his mistakes, machine learning algorithms iteratively refine their models by training on data and learning from the errors they make.

1.3 STORY: "SORTING FRUITS"

ONce upon a time, in a village named DataTown, the townspeople had a peculiar problem. Every day they received huge piles of fruit, but they couldn't quickly tell the difference between ripe and unripe ones. The town had an old manual that described the characteristics of ripe fruits, but it was too time-consuming for everyone to read and the results weren't always accurate.

A young lad named Leo, who was always curious and inventive, decided he wanted to help the village. He took a different approach. Instead of teaching everyone the old manual's way, he decided to observe the fruits that the villagers ate (which were ripe) and those they discarded (which were unripe). He then created a fruit-sorting machine.

At first, his machine was simple. Villagers showed it examples of ripe and unripe fruits. When it saw a fruit, it guessed whether it was ripe or not. If it was wrong, villagers corrected it. Over time, as it saw more and more examples, it got better at telling the difference.

Eventually, the machine could sort the fruits faster and more accurately than anyone in the village using the old manual. The villagers were ecstatic and hailed Leo as a hero. From that day, whenever someone from another village asked about their efficient fruit sorting, DataTown residents would smile and talk about Leo's learning machine.

Figure 1.3: Prompt: A young boy watches others eat fruits in a bright pleasant environment in digital art style.

ANALOGY EXPLANATION

- *DataTown* represents the world filled with vast amounts of data.

- The *pile of fruits* symbolizes data that needs to be classified or understood.

- The *old manual* represents traditional rule-based systems, where everything has to be explicitly defined for a system to function.

- *Leo* is analogous to a machine learning practitioner or scientist.

- The *fruit-sorting machine* represents a machine learning model.

- The *process of showing the machine ripe and unripe fruits* and the machine making guesses stands for training a machine learning model. Just like the machine learns from its mistakes and corrects itself with more data, ML models improve their predictions as they're exposed to more training data.

- The machine getting better over time depicts the iterative nature of training a machine learning model where with each cycle (or epoch), the model gets better.

The story illustrates that machine learning is about teaching machines to learn from data rather than programming them with explicit rules. As they are exposed to more examples (data), they adjust and improve their predictions or classifications, much like how the fruit-sorting machine got better at sorting ripe from unripe fruits.

1.4   EXPLANATION AT THREE LEVELS
OF DEPTH

The following descriptions explain "What is Machine Learning" at three levels of complexity.

SIMPLIFIED

Imagine your brain is like a sponge that soaks up information. When you play a game or read a book multiple times, you get better at it because you learn from what happened before. Machine learning is like giving a computer a mini-brain that helps it learn from playing a game over and over. So, instead of telling the computer every step to win, we just let it play, make mistakes, and learn just like you do!

GENERAL

Machine learning is a type of computer science where we teach computers to learn from data. You know how when you study for a test, you look for patterns in the information, like which topics are most important or which formulas to use when? Similarly, in machine learning, we give computers a lot of data (like past test questions) and let them figure out the patterns. Over time, with more data and practice, the computer gets better at making predictions or decisions, just like you get better at a subject with more study and practice.

DETAILED

Machine learning is a subset of artificial intelligence that emphasizes the development of algorithms that allow computers to evolve behaviors based on empirical data. Essentially, we're trying to develop models that can generalize patterns from large datasets. The goal is to make decisions or predictions without being explicitly programmed to do so. This is achieved through iterative processes where models adjust and optimize their internal parameters when exposed to new data. Different algorithms, ranging from linear regression to deep neural networks, have varying assumptions, strengths, and weaknesses, and their applicability depends on the nature of the data and the problem being addressed. The success of machine learning in diverse areas, from computer vision to natural language processing, hinges on its ability to find and exploit structures in data.

CHAPTER 2

APPLICATIONS OF ML

In the subsequent trio of tales, we explore the diverse 'Applications of Machine Learning.' After each story, we break down its embedded analogies. This is followed by clear, easy-to-understand explanations crafted at three levels of detail simplified, general, and detailed; allowing readers to progressively deepen their understanding.

2.1 STORY: "THE MAGICAL KINGDOM - PREDICTORIA"

In a magical kingdom called Predictoria, problems weren't solved by wizards or warriors, but by seers who could peer into crystal balls. Each seer had a unique crystal ball that showed them different aspects of the future.

Luna, a young seer, had a crystal ball that could show what songs people would want to dance to at the grand annual ball. Every year, she'd gaze into her crystal and curate the perfect playlist that got everyone dancing.

Milo, another seer, had a crystal ball that revealed shadows. These shadows were early signs of illnesses. By looking into his ball, Milo could advise the kingdom's healers on who might fall sick, allowing them to prepare remedies in advance.

Then there was Aria, who had a unique crystal ball. It reflected not the future, but the past. When merchants came with their colorful tapestries, she would glance into her crystal to see if a similar design had been popular in the past, helping merchants know what would sell.

Year after year, Predictoria thrived because of these seers. Their crystals weren't mere tools but were trained through countless observations, ensuring that their visions were as precise as they could be.

ANALOGY EXPLANATION

- *Predictoria* symbolizes our modern world where predictions, based on data, drive many decisions.

- *Seers with crystal balls* represent different machine learning applications.

- *Luna's crystal ball* is akin to *Recommendation Systems*. Platforms like Spotify or Netflix use machine learning to predict and recommend songs, movies, or series that users might like based on their listening or viewing history.

- *Milo's crystal ball* represents *Predictive Healthcare Systems*. Today, machine learning aids in predicting potential health issues by analyzing medical records, genetic data, or even images like X-rays.

- *Aria's crystal ball* is similar to *Market Analysis Tools* in business. Machine learning can analyze past sales data, customer reviews, and more to predict which products might become popular or what kind of services customers might need.

The underlying theme is that like the seers trained their crystal balls through observations, machine learning models are trained on vast amounts of data to make accurate predictions. The better the training (i.e., the more data and the more

Figure 2.1: Prompt: A young seer looking at a crystal ball to predict the future in oil and canvas style.

relevant the data), the better the predictions, ensuring that sectors like entertainment, healthcare, and business can operate more efficiently and effectively.

2.2 STORY: "MIRRA, THE MAGICAL MIRROR"

IN the enchanting land of Predictoria, there was a magical mirror called Mirra. Mirra wasn't your ordinary mirror; she had the power to learn and make predictions.

Every morning, Queen Ada would ask, "Mirra, Mirra on the wall, how should I prepare for the ball?" Mirra would shimmer and shine, showing the Queen what dress to wear based on the expected weather and the guests attending.

In the bustling market square of Predictoria, merchants loved Mirra too. Fisherman Finn would ask, "Mirra, where should I cast my net today?" Mirra would illustrate a part of the ocean where fish patterns had been abundant recently.

Little Mia, a schoolgirl, would approach the mirror before her tests and ask, "Mirra, which topics should I study the most?" The mirror, having observed Mia's past challenges and the common questions teachers asked, would highlight subjects for her to focus on.

Yet, what amazed everyone was Mirra's ability to help Doctor Dara. Whenever Dara was puzzled by a patient's symptoms, he'd ask, "Mirra, what might ail this patient?" The magical mirror would then display potential diagnoses, based on patterns from countless past patients.

As years went by, Predictoria thrived. Not because of magic, but because of the learning power of Mirra. While she sometimes made mistakes, continuous learning from everyone around made her an essential part of Predictoria.

Figure 2.2: Prompt: A person looking at a magical mirror in a bright colorful room in digital art style.

ANALOGY EXPLANATION

- *Predictoria*: Represents the world filled with vast amounts of data and the potential for predictions.

- *Mirra, the magical mirror*: Symbolizes a machine learning system. It gathers data, learns from it, and makes predictions or suggestions based on patterns it recognizes.

- *Queen Ada's ball preparation*: Demonstrates recommendation systems, similar to how platforms suggest movies or products based on past preferences and other factors.

- *Fisherman Finn's fishing spot*: Illustrates predictive analytics, akin to how businesses might forecast sales or stock demands.

- *Mia's study topics*: Represents personalized learning platforms which analyze a student's strengths and weaknesses, offering tailored study suggestions.

- *Doctor Dara's diagnoses*: Depicts medical diagnosis tools that analyze symptoms, medical images, or genomic data to aid in identifying potential diseases.

The story illustrates that machine learning has a wide range of applications, from personal recommendations to business optimizations and even critical tasks like medical diagnoses. Just like Mirra, machine learning systems continuously improve as they're exposed to more data, becoming more accurate and valuable over time.

2.3 STORY: "MAGICAL KINGDOM OF ALGORITHMA"

In the magical kingdom of Algorithmia, there was a renowned wizard named Algor. Algor wasn't like other wizards; instead of casting spells, he crafted enchanted mirrors. Each mirror had a unique purpose.

One mirror, when gazed upon, would reflect not your current image but how you'd look in different outfits. Tailors loved it, as it helped them design the perfect attire for anyone without the need for tedious fittings.

Another mirror in his collection showed the health of the crops in a field. Farmers would peer into it and, instead of seeing their reflection, they'd witness which parts of their land were flourishing and which needed attention.

Yet, another exceptional mirror he designed was for the royal guards. Whenever a threat approached the kingdom, the mirror would predict its direction and help strategize the defense.

Over time, Algor's mirrors became essential to the kingdom's day-to-day functioning. They seemed magical, but in reality, each mirror was observing, learning from patterns, and helping make decisions. And so, the legend of Algor and his insightful mirrors spread across lands, making him the most sought-after wizard in history.

ANALOGY EXPLANATION

In this story, the kingdom of Algorithmia represents the modern world, and the wizard Algor symbolizes the inventors and scientists behind machine learning.

- *Mirror for Outfit Prediction:* This represents recommendation systems. Just as the mirror showed individuals how they'd look in various outfits, recommendation systems in online shopping platforms suggest products based on what we've browsed or bought before.

- *Mirror for Crop Health:* This stands for machine learning in agriculture. Precision agriculture uses machine learning to analyze data from satellite images and sensors in the field, predicting which areas need water, pesticides, or other care, much like the mirror showed which parts of the land were flourishing.

Figure 2.3: Prompt: A person looking at magical mirrors and seeing a different image in each mirror in digital art style.

- *Mirror for Defense Strategy:* This signifies predictive analytics in security or threat detection. Systems in cybersecurity use machine learning to detect anomalies and predict potential threats based on patterns, similar to how the mirror could predict threats to the kingdom.

Algor's mirrors learned and evolved based on the patterns they observed, echoing the very essence of machine learning applications in diverse sectors today.

2.4 EXPLANATION AT THREE LEVELS OF DEPTH

The following descriptions explain "Applications of Machine Learning" in three levels of detail.

SIMPLIFIED

Imagine if:
- A toy could recognize and greet you when you came near.
- A robot could clean up your room without being told exactly where each toy goes.
- A computer game got smarter and adjusted to how you play to keep things fun and challenging.

All these magical things can happen because of something called machine learning! It's like teaching computers to get better at tasks by practicing them.

GENERAL

Machine learning is like a super-powered tool for computers. With its help:

- Websites like Netflix or Spotify can suggest movies or songs you might like, based on what you've watched or listened to before.

- Your phone's camera can automatically detect faces and focus on them.

- Video games can adapt to your playing style and make the game more challenging and interesting.

- Doctors can use it to help detect diseases early by analyzing medical images.

In short, machine learning helps computers make decisions based on patterns and data they've seen before, rather than relying on specific instructions.

DETAILED

Machine learning has deeply penetrated various domains due to its ability to extract patterns from vast amounts of data and make predictive decisions. Some advanced applications include:

- *Financial Forecasting:* Algorithmic trading strategies employ machine learning models to predict market trends based on historical data, helping institutions maximize returns and minimize risks.

- *Natural Language Processing:* Sentiment analysis, translation, and chatbots utilize machine learning to understand and generate human language in a contextually relevant manner.

- *Healthcare:* Advanced diagnostic tools utilize machine learning to detect anomalies in medical images, such as MRIs or X-rays, sometimes catching nuances human eyes might miss.

- *Autonomous Systems:* Self-driving cars use machine learning for tasks like object detection, decision-making, and path planning.

- *Research:* In areas such as genomics, machine learning assists in predicting protein structures or understanding the complexities of gene expressions.

These applications require nuanced understanding and rigorous evaluations, given the critical nature of decisions they inform. The algorithm's choice, data preprocessing methods, and validation metrics are vital components in the deployment of these systems.

CHAPTER 3

TYPES OF MACHINE LEARNING

In the upcoming trio of tales, we delve into the distinct 'Types of Machine Learning', encompassing supervised, unsupervised, and reinforcement learning. Each story unfolds with a clarification of its symbolic nuances. Following these narratives, straightforward interpretations are presented and thoughtfully curated at three levels of complexity to progressively deepen the understanding of the readers.

3.1 STORY: "THE TALE OF THE THREE APPRENTICES"

IN the land of Technos, Master Maestro, the revered blacksmith, was known for crafting the most intricate and unique artifacts. One day, he decided to take in three apprentices: Alvin, Bella, and Charlie, each to be taught in a manner that best suited their strengths.

Alvin was handed a toolset and a plethora of blueprints. Master Maestro instructed, "Learn by following these designs to the dot.

Replicate each artifact precisely." And so, day after day, Alvin meticulously crafted items, always referencing the designs he'd been provided.

Bella was given a slightly different task. She was handed a half-finished artifact and the toolset, along with a description of what the final product should be. "Use your skills to complete these items," Master Maestro directed. Bella would carefully study the partial item, determine what was missing, and proceed to complete it.

Lastly, *Charlie* was presented with just the tools and materials but no blueprints or samples. "Craft something new, something the world has never seen," Master Maestro challenged. Charlie, though initially daunted, soon began experimenting, iterating, and refining, eventually producing masterpieces of his own.

ANALOGY EXPLANATION

In this tale, Master Maestro's blacksmith shop represents the world of machine learning, and his teaching methods align with the three primary types of machine learning.

- *Alvin and Supervised Learning:* Just as Alvin was given blueprints to replicate the artifacts, supervised learning uses labeled data to train models. The model 'learns' from the provided data and its corresponding output, much like Alvin learned from the blueprints.

- *Bella and Semi-Supervised/Unsupervised Learning:* Bella's task, where she had to study a half-finished artifact and figure out its completion, is akin to semi-supervised learning, where models are trained on a mix of labeled and unlabeled data. If she had only the materials and a hint or pattern recognition task without specific blueprints, it would resemble unsupervised learning where the model identifies structures or patterns in the data without explicit guidance.

Figure 3.1: Prompt: A person working to create an artifact using a toolset and a plethora of sample blueprints in oil and canvas style

- *Charlie and Reinforcement Learning:* Charlie's challenge to create something entirely new, through trial and error, mirrors reinforcement learning. Here, an agent (like Charlie) interacts with an environment (his tools and materials) to maximize a reward (crafting a unique artifact), refining its strategies over multiple attempts.

Through the endeavors of the three apprentices, we see how different types of machine learning approaches handle data and tasks, each with its distinct charm and application.

3.2 STORY: "THREE SIBLING WIZARDS"

IN the mystical land of Computerra, three sibling wizards – Supervisus, Unsupervisus, and Reinforca – ruled different realms, each using their unique style of magic to maintain harmony and balance.

Supervisus, the eldest, always liked guidance. He'd summon creatures, but only when the villagers gave him a picture and name of the creature they desired. With this information, he'd conjure the exact creature they had in mind. Over time, he became a master at crafting creatures when given a hint of what was expected.

Unsupervisus, the free-spirited middle child, preferred discovery. He'd summon creatures without any direct requests, instead analyzing what the environment might need. He looked at the shadows, the winds, the mood of the forest, and conjured beings that seemed right. It was more about understanding patterns and the inherent nature of the world.

The youngest, Reinforca, was an adventurer. He learned by trial and error. He'd summon a creature, send it into the village, and see if the villagers cheered or booed. If they cheered, he'd

Figure 3.2: Prompt: Three Sibling Wizards performing magic in oil and canvas style.

remember and make more of the same. If they booed, he'd adjust and try something different next time. Over time, he became better, remembering what the villagers loved and what they didn't.

The combined magic of these three wizards made Computerra a balanced and thriving land.

ANALOGY EXPLANATION

In this story, Computerra symbolizes the world of machine learning, and the three wizards represent different types of learning algorithms.

- *Supervisus*: He represents *Supervised Learning*, where models are trained on a labeled dataset, meaning they're provided with input-output pairs. Just like Supervisus needs a picture (input) and a name (output) to conjure the creature, supervised learning algorithms need labeled data to learn and make predictions.

- *Unsupervisus*: He signifies *Unsupervised Learning*. In this type of machine learning, algorithms work on unlabeled data, aiming to discover the inherent patterns or structures within, just as Unsupervisus analyses the environment to determine which creature to summon.

- *Reinforca*: He stands for *Reinforcement Learning*, where an agent learns by interacting with an environment, receiving feedback (rewards or penalties) for actions, and then refining its strategies accordingly. Reinforca's method of summoning creatures based on villagers' reactions mirrors this approach.

3.3   STORY: "THE ENCHANTED FOREST OF LEARNICA"

ONCE upon a time in the enchanted forest of Learnica, there were three magical creatures, each guarding a distinct path that travelers could take.

The first creature was a wise old owl named Superviso. Whenever travelers came to the forest, Superviso would show them a series of pictures, telling them, "This is a tree... This is a river... This is a mountain..." By showing and naming each item, he ensured travelers knew what to expect on their journey.

The second creature was a playful squirrel named Unsuperviso. Instead of showing pictures, she scattered a mix of nuts, leaves, and berries on the ground. Travelers would group them based on similarities. "Look! All the pine nuts are together, and all the maple leaves are over there!" they'd exclaim, finding their own patterns and understanding.

Lastly, there was a mysterious fox named Reinforco. He didn't show pictures or scatter items. Instead, he set up a series of challenges with hidden rewards. Travelers would try different strategies, sometimes succeeding, sometimes failing. When they found a reward, they'd remember their steps, learning through trial and error.

Over time, adventurers in Learnica came to understand that each path offered a unique way to understand the world, guided by the forest's magical creatures.

ANALOGY EXPLANATION

- *Superviso, the Owl:* This represents *Supervised Learning*. Just as the owl provides travelers with labeled data (naming each item), supervised learning uses labeled datasets to train algorithms. The model learns from the data, making future predictions based on this training.

- *Unsuperviso, the Squirrel:* Symbolic of *Unsupervised Learning*. The squirrel doesn't provide any labels, just like unsupervised learning where algorithms sift through data and classify or group it based on patterns or similarities, without prior labeling.

- *Reinforco, the Fox:* This embodies *Reinforcement Learning*. In reinforcement learning, an agent (like the travelers) makes decisions by taking actions in an environment to maximize a reward. The learning process involves exploration (trying out strategies) and exploitation (using strategies that are known to yield rewards).

The Enchanted Forest of Learnica, with its three magical creatures, provides a picturesque view of the three primary

Figure 3.3: Prompt: Three magical animals: a wise owl, a playful squirrel and mysterious fox in oil and canvas style.

machine learning paradigms, making them easier to comprehend and remember.

3.4 EXPLANATION AT THREE LEVELS OF DEPTH

The following descriptions explain "Types of Machine Learning" in three levels of depth.

SIMPLIFIED

Imagine you're trying to teach a robot to do things:
- **Teaching with Labels:** If you show your robot a ball and say, "This is a ball," and then you show a car and say, "This is a car," you're teaching it by giving names or labels to things. That's like one way computers learn, and it's called "Supervised Learning."
- **Letting the Robot Sort:** Now, if you show your robot a bunch of items without telling it what they are, and it groups all balls together and all cars together by itself, that's another way called "Unsupervised Learning."
- **Learning with Rewards:** Suppose you create a game where your robot gets a small treat every time it does something right. It tries many things and learns from mistakes to earn its treats. This method of learning by trial and reward is called "Reinforcement Learning."

GENERAL

Machine learning is a way for computers to learn and make decisions:
- **Supervised Learning:** This is like using a study guide with all the answers. You're given a set of data where the answer or result is already known, and the computer learns from this to

make predictions for new data. For example, if we teach it with pictures of cats and tell it they are cats, it learns to identify new cat pictures.

- **Unsupervised Learning:** Here, it's like trying to sort things without being told any categories. The computer gets data without any labels and tries to find patterns or groupings on its own. For instance, given a bunch of photos, it might group together all photos with blue skies or all photos with trees.

- **Reinforcement Learning:** This is similar to learning a new video game. As you play, you learn from your mistakes and successes. Similarly, in reinforcement learning, the computer or 'agent' learns by interacting with an environment and receiving rewards or penalties based on its actions.

DETAILED

Machine learning encompasses algorithms that enable computers to improve their performance over time. The three main types are:

- **Supervised Learning:** Algorithms are trained on a labeled dataset, meaning the outcome variable (or "label") is known. The model makes predictions based on this training and is then tested on unseen data to evaluate its accuracy. Common algorithms include regression, classification, and neural networks.

- **Unsupervised Learning:** Here, the algorithm is given data without explicit instructions on what to do with it. The system tries to learn the patterns and the structure from the data without any labeled responses to guide the learning process. Techniques often used include clustering and association.

- **Reinforcement Learning:** In this paradigm, an agent learns by interacting with its environment, receiving feedback in the form of rewards or penalties. The learning process involves exploration (trying out strategies) and exploitation (using strategies that are known to yield rewards). Markov Decision Processes often underpin the mathematical structure of these problems.

CHAPTER 4

MACHINE LEARNING PROCESS

In the next trio of tales, we delve into the 'Machine Learning Process.' After each story, we unpack the allegories woven within. Subsequently, we present clear explanations of the topic in three different levels of depth for a progressive understanding.

4.1   STORY: "THE GREAT POTION MASTER'S QUEST"

IN the mystical land of DataLandia, there was a renowned potion master named Lyrus. Lyrus was given the formidable task of concocting a potion that could make crops grow twice as fast, a solution desperately needed due to an impending famine.

1. *Gathering Rare Ingredients:* Lyrus started by collecting ingredients from various parts of the land. He visited forests, caves, and even dove deep into the oceans. He knew that the better and more diverse his ingredients, the more potent his potion could be.

2. *Old Recipe Books:* Returning to his lab, Lyrus consulted his ancient recipe books, identifying which ingredients had historically

worked well together. He was determined to use these old recipes as a starting point but knew innovation was necessary.

3. *Experimentation:* For weeks, Lyrus mixed and matched the ingredients in varying proportions, noting down the results of each combination. Some mixtures burned, some turned to ice, and some simply evaporated. But slowly, a pattern began to emerge.

4. *Testing on a Small Farm:* Before unveiling his potion to the entire kingdom, Lyrus chose a small farm for testing. He observed the crops day and night, adjusting his potion's formulation based on real-world feedback.

5. *Tweaking and Perfecting:* Based on the results from the small farm, Lyrus went back to his lab, tweaking the potion to improve its efficiency.

6. *Widespread Use:* Finally, confident in his concoction, Lyrus introduced it to the entire realm of DataLandia. Crops flourished, the famine was averted, and Lyrus was celebrated as a hero.

ANALOGY EXPLANATION

1. *Gathering Rare Ingredients:* This is analogous to *Data Collection.* In machine learning, collecting diverse and relevant data is crucial for training a model effectively.

2. *Old Recipe Books:* Lyrus consulting old recipes signifies the *Review of Existing Models or Research.* Before creating a new machine learning model, it's beneficial to understand previous work in the domain.

3. *Experimentation:* This symbolizes the *Training Phase* of the machine learning process. Different algorithms and hyperparameters are tried out on the training dataset to develop the most effective model.

4. *Testing on a Small Farm:* Represents the *Validation Phase.* Before deploying a model in a real-world scenario, it's tested on a separate validation set to gauge its performance.

Figure 4.1: Prompt: An old man mixing up ingredients to create a potion in oil and canvas style

5. *Tweaking and Perfecting:* This step mirrors the *Model Optimization* process, where the model is refined based on validation results to enhance its accuracy or efficiency.

6. *Widespread Use:* Finally, rolling out the potion to all of DataLandia signifies *Deployment.* Once satisfied with a model's performance, it's put into production, serving real-world applications.

Lyrus' journey in concocting the perfect potion parallels the steps involved in crafting an effective machine learning model, emphasizing the importance of iteration and feedback at every stage.

4.2   STORY: "THE BAKER'S EXPERIMENT IN FLAVOR TOWN"

IN the bustling town of Flavor, there was a passionate baker named Lina who was known for her scrumptious cookies. Yet, Lina wasn't content. She dreamt of crafting the ultimate cookie that all of Flavor would love.

1. *Collection:* Lina began by gathering all the ingredients she could find. She traveled far and wide, collecting unique spices, exotic fruits, and various types of chocolate. Her shop was filled with ingredients from all over the world.

2. *Cleaning and Preparation:* However, some ingredients were not fit for her cookies. The overripe fruits, stale nuts, and hardened chocolate had to be sorted out. She then organized her ingredients, ensuring each was of top quality and ready to use.

3. *Experiment:* Armed with her ingredients and a notebook, Lina began experimenting. She tried different combinations, noting down how much of each ingredient she used for every batch.

4. *Feedback Loop:* Every evening, she would set up a stall in the town square, offering samples of her experimental cookies. The

townspeople would taste and rate them. Lina keenly observed their reactions, noting their preferences.

5. *Adjustments:* Using the feedback, Lina adjusted her recipes. If a cookie was too sweet, she reduced sugar. Too dry? She'd add more butter.

6. *Perfecting the Recipe:* After many iterations, using the feedback and her notes, Lina discovered the ultimate cookie recipe that was adored by almost everyone in Flavor.

7. *Final Product:* The day arrived when Lina, confident in her creation, unveiled the "Flavor Bliss Cookie." It was an instant sensation, becoming a cherished treat for both locals and visitors.

ANALOGY EXPLANATION

1. *Collection:* This represents *Data Collection*. Just as Lina gathered ingredients, in machine learning, we gather data relevant to the problem.

2. *Cleaning and Preparation:* Analogous to *Data Cleaning and Preprocessing*. Data, like raw ingredients, can often be messy or inappropriate for direct use. It needs to be cleaned, organized, and sometimes transformed.

3. *Experiment:* This stage mirrors *Model Training*. Lina tried different combinations of ingredients, akin to training a machine learning model with different parameters and algorithms on the collected data.

4. *Feedback Loop:* The townspeople's feedback represents *Validation*. By validating the model (or in this case, the cookie recipe) on a separate set of data (or different townspeople), we can gauge its performance.

5. *Adjustments:* Lina tweaking her recipe based on feedback aligns with *Model Tuning*. Once we know how the model performs, we adjust its parameters to improve its predictions.

6. *Perfecting the Recipe:* This embodies *Iterative Training and Validation*. Machine learning isn't a one-shot process; it requires

Figure 4.2: Prompt: A baker cooking a delicious cookie in oil and canvas style.

multiple iterations to refine the model, much like Lina's pursuit of the perfect cookie.

7. *Final Product:* The "Flavor Bliss Cookie" symbolizes the *Final Trained Model*. Once optimized, the model is ready for deployment and broader application, just like Lina's cookie being sold to the public.

4.3 STORY: "THE QUEST FOR THE PERFECT POTION"

IN the magical town of Algoria, young apprentice Luna was given a task by her master, Elder Orion: to brew a potion that can make flowers bloom instantly. Luna was determined but unsure where to start.

Step 1: The Gathering Luna began by gathering various ingredients from the vast library of herbs, minerals, and enchanted waters. Each ingredient represented knowledge, some widely known and some obscure.

Step 2: The Recipe She then recalled stories of past potions and decided to start with a base recipe, tweaking it based on her intuition. She was creating a guide, or algorithm, on how to combine the ingredients.

Step 3: The Trials Pouring tiny amounts into small vials, she tested different concoctions. Some had no effect; some caused the flowers to wilt. But a few made tiny buds appear.

Step 4: Feedback from Nature Every time a potion was tested, nature provided feedback. The blooming or wilting of a flower was like a signal, guiding Luna's next steps.

Step 5: Perfecting the Brew With each attempt, Luna refined her recipe, noting down the exact measures and sequences. She continually improved, adapting based on what she learned from previous attempts.

Figure 4.3: Prompt: A man delicately dispensing droplets of potion onto a radiant, thriving flower, in oil and canvas style.

Step 6: Validation After several attempts, Luna believed she had the perfect potion. To ensure it wasn't a fluke, she tested it on a new set of flowers she hadn't used before. To her delight, they bloomed instantly!

Elder Orion, witnessing the entire process, smiled and said, "Just as you've learned to brew the perfect potion through trial, observation, and refinement, so do the machines in the world beyond learn from data."

ANALOGY EXPLANATION

1. *The Gathering:* This symbolizes the *Data Collection* phase in machine learning. Just as Luna collected ingredients, we gather data from various sources to train our model.

2. *The Recipe:* Represents the *Algorithm Selection* phase. Luna's choice of starting with a base recipe is similar to choosing an initial algorithm based on past knowledge or intuition.

3. *The Trials:* This mirrors the *Training* phase, where different combinations (or parameters) are tried out to see how well the algorithm performs.

4. *Feedback from Nature:* Corresponds to the *Evaluation* phase in machine learning. The blooming or wilting of flowers is akin to the feedback we get when we assess our model's predictions against actual outcomes.

5. *Perfecting the Brew:* This is the *Optimization* phase, where the algorithm is refined based on feedback, just as Luna tweaked her potion recipe.

6. *Validation:* Luna's final test on a new set of flowers stands for the *Validation* phase in machine learning, ensuring the model works well on previously unseen data.

Elder Orion's closing remark ties the entire analogy together, drawing a parallel between Luna's quest and the machine learning process.

4.4 EXPLANATION AT THREE LEVELS OF DEPTH

The following descriptions explain the "Machine Learning Process" at three levels of complexity.

SIMPLIFIED

Imagine a boy is trying to teach his pet robot how to recognize and sort your toys:

1. **Collecting Toys:** First, he gathers all your toys in one place.

2. **Showing Examples:** Then, he shows the robot some toys and tells it their names. "This is a teddy bear, this is a toy car."

3. **Practice Time:** The robot tries to sort the toys based on what was taught. It might make mistakes, but that's okay!

4. **Test Time:** Now, the boy brings out toys it hasn't seen before and asks it to sort them. If it does well, you can let it sort your whole toy box!

5. **Better Sorting:** If the robot gets confused or makes errors, the boy shows it again and corrects it to help it understand better.

GENERAL

Machine learning is like teaching a computer to make decisions based on data:

1. **Data Collection:** Just as you need textbooks to study, a machine needs data to learn. So, we gather a lot of data on what we want the computer to learn.

2. **Training:** Using part of this data, we 'train' the computer. It's like giving it lessons on the topic.

3. **Validation:** Once trained, we check how well the computer is doing using a different part of the data. Think of this as a practice quiz before the final exam.

4. **Testing:** Now, we evaluate the computer using new data it hasn't seen before. This is the final exam to see how well it's learned.

5. **Model Optimization:** If the computer doesn't perform well on the test, we adjust and refine its learning to improve accuracy.

DETAILED

Machine Learning entails the systematic application of algorithms to teach computers to make decisions from data:

1. **Data Collection & Preprocessing:** The first step involves collecting a substantial dataset relevant to the problem domain. This data is then preprocessed to handle missing values, outliers, and potential noise.

2. **Feature Engineering:** Extracting relevant features and transforming data into a usable format is essential. This can significantly influence the predictive power of the model.

3. **Training:** A suitable algorithm is chosen based on the problem type (classification, regression, clustering, etc.) and is trained using a subset of the data.

4. **Validation:** The model's hyperparameters are tuned and its performance is evaluated using a separate validation set. This iterative process aims to prevent overfitting and ensure generalization.

5. **Testing:** The finalized model's efficacy is assessed on a test dataset to understand its real-world applicability.

6. **Deployment & Monitoring:** Once satisfactory performance is achieved, the model is deployed in a production environment. Continuous monitoring ensures the model remains relevant and adapts to changing data patterns.

The machine learning process is cyclical and often requires multiple iterations before achieving a model with the desired performance metrics.

CHAPTER 5

ESSENTIAL MATHEMATICS

In the next trio of tales, we delve into the 'Essential Mathematics for Machine Learning.' After each narrative, we unpack the metaphors interwoven within. Conclusively, we present three clear interpretations of the subject, tailored to resonate with readers.

5.1 STORY: "THE MAGIC TOWER OF NUMBERS"

I N the vibrant town of Numerica, there stood a grand tower known as the Magic Tower of Numbers. This wasn't an ordinary tower; it was said that those who could navigate its levels could harness the power of prediction and make wise decisions.

1. *The Ground Floor - Arithmetic Plaza:* Young Tim entered the tower and found himself surrounded by basic numbers and operations. Addition, subtraction, multiplication, and division danced around. It was a foundation, and Tim quickly realized he couldn't ascend without mastering these basics.

2. *The First Floor - Algebraic Alcove:* As he climbed higher, letters joined numbers. These weren't just any letters; they represented unknown quantities. Equations and formulas swirled, showing

relationships. With a spark of realization, Tim saw that this level taught him how to find patterns and relationships between numbers.

3. *The Second Floor - Geometry Garden:* Here, Tim was greeted by shapes, lines, and angles. He realized that understanding space and dimensions was crucial. As he solved problems involving distances and areas, he began to see the world in a new dimension.

4. *The Third Floor - Calculus Chamber:* This level was a realm of motion and change. It taught Tim how to predict future movements by understanding the present and past. Differential equations became his tools, and integration his technique for accumulating knowledge.

5. *The Fourth Floor - Probability Parlor:* In this mysterious room, Tim encountered chances and uncertainties. He learned the art of making educated guesses about future events based on available data.

6. *The Penthouse - Linear Algebra Lounge:* At the pinnacle of the tower, vectors and matrices reigned supreme. They helped Tim transform vast amounts of information into comprehensible forms, making large-scale predictions possible.

Having navigated the tower, Tim emerged with newfound knowledge, ready to use mathematics to understand and shape his world.

ANALOGY EXPLANATION

1. *Arithmetic Plaza:* Just as arithmetic is fundamental to all of mathematics, basic mathematical operations are essential for any machine learning task.

2. *Algebraic Alcove:* Algebra helps in understanding relationships and patterns, much like how machine learning identifies patterns in data.

Figure 5.1: Prompt: A huge round shape brick tower with six distinct sections on top of each other, in oil and canvas style.

3. *Geometry Garden:* Geometry aids in spatial understanding, and in machine learning, especially in areas like computer vision, spatial relationships are key.

4. *Calculus Chamber:* Calculus is the study of change, and in machine learning, understanding change can help predict future outcomes, like in time-series analysis.

5. *Probability Parlor:* Machine learning often deals with uncertain outcomes and predictions, making probability an essential component.

6. *Linear Algebra Lounge:* Linear algebra, with its vectors and matrices, is fundamental in handling large datasets and transformations in machine learning.

In essence, the Magic Tower of Numbers represents the layers of mathematical knowledge that are pivotal in mastering machine learning.

5.2 STORY: "THE QUEST FOR THE MYSTIC PRISM"

IN the enchanting town of Mathema, young Ada had always been in awe of the fabled Mystic Prism. Legend said that this prism could refract light into patterns revealing hidden truths of the universe. Ada, aspiring to be the town's leading sage, decided she must decipher the prism's mysteries.

1. *Foundation Stones:* Before embarking on her quest, Ada visited the Oracle of Basics. The Oracle handed her three stones labeled "Linear Algebra," "Calculus," and "Probability." "These are your foundational tools," the Oracle said. "They will guide your understanding."

2. *Valley of Vectors:* First, Ada entered the Valley of Vectors. Using the Linear Algebra stone, she understood the significance of

directions and magnitudes, helping her navigate through the maze of lines and planes.

3. *Mount Differentia:* As she ascended the treacherous terrains of Mount Differentia, Ada utilized her Calculus stone. It helped her comprehend the changes in terrains and predict the paths she should take to avoid pitfalls.

4. *Forest of Chance:* To cross the dense Forest of Chance, she turned to her Probability stone. It enabled her to anticipate uncertain events, like rain or creature movements, thus assisting her to make informed choices.

After crossing these lands, Ada finally reached the Mystic Prism. As she shone light through it, beautiful patterns emerged. She now had the tools to interpret them, understanding the universe's hidden truths.

ANALOGY EXPLANATION

1. *Foundation Stones:* These represent the three essential mathematical domains required in machine learning. Just as Ada needed tools to start her quest, any machine learning enthusiast needs these fundamental concepts.

2. *Valley of Vectors:* Linear Algebra, especially the understanding of vectors and matrices, is pivotal for handling and interpreting data, akin to how Ada navigated the valley.

3. *Mount Differentia:* Calculus helps in understanding changes and making predictions, much like how Ada used it to understand the shifting terrains. In machine learning, calculus is crucial for optimization problems, such as gradient descent.

4. *Forest of Chance:* Probability and statistics guide decisions made under uncertainty. Ada's journey through the forest mirrors how machine learning algorithms deal with uncertain data and make predictions.

The journey to understanding machine learning, much like Ada's quest, requires the mastery of certain mathematical tools.

Figure 5.2: Prompt: A prism, at the hand of a man, refracts light into patterns in oil and canvas style

These tools empower enthusiasts to decipher complex patterns and draw meaningful insights.

5.3 Story: "The Kingdom of MathLandia"

IN the enchanting kingdom of MathLandia, the reigning Queen Ada was renowned for her wisdom. But not many knew that her wisdom was rooted in her understanding of three sacred pillars of knowledge.

1. *The Pillar of Shapes and Spaces:* In the heart of the kingdom stood a towering pillar, a testament to geometry's power. Here, every shape and size from the tiniest dot to the vast expanses of space was known. It was believed that understanding these shapes and spaces could help decipher the patterns of the stars and the lands.

2. *The Pillar of Chance:* Located near the river of randomness, this shimmering pillar represented statistics. Fishermen casting their nets into the river never knew what they'd catch, much like the unpredictability in life. But with the power of this pillar, Queen Ada could predict the best times and spots to cast the net, optimizing the catch.

3. *The Pillar of Relationships:* Standing atop a hill, this pillar was intricately carved with various symbols, representing algebra and calculus. It illuminated how things in the kingdom related to one another, changing and influencing each other over time.

One day, a challenge arose: a maze that changed its path daily. To navigate it, Queen Ada didn't rely on magic but turned to the three pillars. Using geometry, she understood the maze's structure; with statistics, she predicted its changing patterns; and through calculus, she discerned how its paths evolved over time.

Figure 5.3: Prompt: A queen holding three sacred pillars in her hand in oil and canvas style.

Guided by the essential math, Queen Ada conquered the maze, showing her kingdom that with the right knowledge, any challenge can be surmounted.

ANALOGY EXPLANATION

1. *The Pillar of Shapes and Spaces:* This signifies *Linear Algebra and Geometry,* foundational for understanding data structures, spaces, and transformations in machine learning.

2. *The Pillar of Chance:* This symbolizes *Probability and Statistics*, which are vital for understanding data distributions, making predictions, and evaluating machine learning models.

3. *The Pillar of Relationships:* Represents *Calculus and Optimization*, as understanding change and the rate of change is essential in tweaking and improving machine learning models, ensuring they perform at their best.

Queen Ada's use of the three pillars to navigate the maze demonstrates how essential these mathematical concepts are in tackling and solving complex problems in machine learning.

5.4 Explanation at Three Levels of Depth

The following descriptions explain "Essential Mathematics for Machine Learning" in three levels of detail.

Simplified

Essential math for machine learning is like the toolbox a builder needs to construct a house. Just as a builder uses different tools for different tasks, in machine learning, we use certain math tools to help computers learn from data and make decisions.

General

Machine learning is a way for computers to learn from data, just like you learn from your textbooks. Now, there are three main types of math that help in this:

1. **Shapes and Spaces:** Think about it as **Linear Algebra and Geometry**. Just like you'd plot points on a graph in math class, computers use this to understand and organize data.

2. **Playing the Odds:** This is **Probability and Statistics**. You know when you try to guess the likelihood of it raining tomorrow? Computers use this math to make their own educated guesses from data.

3. **Change Over Time:** Remember studying how things increase or decrease in math, like graphs that go up and down? This is **Calculus**. It helps computers understand how data changes and how best to adapt to those changes.

Together, these math topics help a computer take in data, understand it, and then make smart decisions!

Detailed

Machine learning, a subfield of artificial intelligence, involves algorithms that allow computers to learn from and make decisions based on data. The foundational mathematics for this domain consists of:

1. **Linear Algebra and Geometry:** These provide the frameworks to represent data in multi-dimensional spaces, essential for most machine learning algorithms. Concepts like vectors, matrices, and transformations are pivotal.

2. **Probability and Statistics:** These are vital for understanding data distributions, and inference, and for many machine learning techniques like Bayesian inference and Maximum Likelihood Estimation. It assists in making probabilistic predictions and understanding the underlying uncertainties.

3. **Calculus and Optimization:** A substantial part of machine learning is about optimization—finding the best model or parameters for a given task. This is often done using techniques from calculus, like gradient descent, to adjust model parameters in iterative refinement processes.

A rigorous understanding of these mathematical frameworks is imperative for developing, analyzing, and refining sophisticated machine-learning algorithms.

CHAPTER 6

SUPERVISED LEARNING

In the upcoming three stories, we'll delve into 'Supervised Learning in Machine Learning.' After each narrative, we'll decode the analogies within. Then, we provide straightforward explanations at three levels of complexity enabling readers to gradually enhance their comprehension.

6.1 STORY: "THE ART TEACHER AND THE YOUNG PRODIGY"

IN the quaint town of Algorville, there was a famed art school known for producing exceptional painters. One day, a young prodigy named Leo joined the school, touted for his innate talent but lacking in refined skills.

Master Picasso, the school's most revered teacher, decided to take Leo under his wing. On their first day, Master Picasso placed a beautiful apple on a table and painted a meticulous rendition of it. Handing Leo a similar canvas and palette, he asked him to replicate the painting.

At first, Leo's renditions were slightly off – the shape wasn't quite right, and the colors were somewhat different. But every time Leo finished, Master Picasso would point out the discrepancies, guiding him on what needed correction.

This process continued for days. Leo would paint, Master Picasso would provide feedback, and Leo would make corrections based on the feedback. Over time, Leo's paintings became near replicas of Master Picasso's, capturing the apple's intricate details and rich colors.

Eventually, Leo's training progressed to the point that when given new subjects to paint - whether it was a vase of flowers or a bustling market scene - he could paint them with stunning accuracy, having learned the principles of art through the guidance of his master.

ANALOGY EXPLANATION

In this story, the process of teaching Leo to paint accurately under the guidance of Master Picasso mirrors *Supervised Learning*:

1. *Master Picasso and Leo:* Master Picasso is the algorithm or model (like Leo) that's being trained. The expertly painted apple by Master Picasso serves as the "correct answer" or the labeled data in machine learning.

2. *The Painting Process:* Every time Leo tries to replicate the painting and receives feedback, it's akin to a model making a prediction and then getting corrected based on a comparison with the actual, known output (label).

3. *Feedback and Corrections:* Master Picasso's feedback is analogous to the loss or error function in supervised learning. By understanding where he went wrong and adjusting, Leo is optimizing his approach, similar to how algorithms adjust their internal parameters to get better results.

4. *New Subjects:* Once trained with enough feedback, Leo could paint new subjects accurately. Similarly, a supervised model, once trained on labeled data, can make accurate predictions on new, unseen data.

Figure 6.1: Prompt: An old painter showing and painting a young painter how to paint in oil and canvas style

6.2   STORY: "THE ARCHER AND THE BULLSEYE"

IN the quaint town of Algoria, young Mia had a dream. She aspired to become the finest archer, a title held for generations by Master Orion. Orion, known for his unmatched skill, didn't achieve greatness overnight. His secret? A unique training technique passed down through ages.

When Mia approached him, eager to learn, he handed her a bow, an arrow, and placed a blindfold around her eyes. He then set up a target - the bullseye. Mia was puzzled, "How can I hit the target I can't see?"

Master Orion, with a smile, guided her hand to draw the bow and let the arrow fly. As expected, it missed. Orion made Mia take note of the sound, direction, and distance it missed by. Again, he adjusted her stance, aim, and posture, all the while offering gentle corrections. With every attempt, Mia's arrows got closer to the target, guided by Orion's feedback.

After many tries, Mia removed the blindfold. To her surprise, even though her initial shots were off, she now possessed the instinct and skill to hit the bullseye consistently. Under the master's watchful eye and constant guidance, she had internalized the skill.

ANALOGY EXPLANATION

In this story, Mia represents a machine learning model, and the arrows are the predictions it makes. The bullseye is the correct answer or the desired outcome. Master Orion embodies the training data with labeled examples (or the "teacher").

- *Blindfolded Mia:* A new model starts without prior knowledge, similar to Mia being blindfolded, uncertain of where the target is.

Figure 6.2: Prompt: A young archer learning how to use bow and arrow while a blindfold is placed around her eyes in oil and canvas style

- *Mia's Attempts:* These are the model's predictions. In the beginning, they might be way off, but they get refined over time.

- *Orion's Guidance:* Just as Master Orion provides feedback and corrections, in supervised learning, the model gets feedback about how off its predictions are from the actual outcomes (labels). The "distance" and "direction" of the missed shots represent the error or loss the model incurs, and the feedback helps adjust the model's parameters.

- *Hitting the Bullseye:* As Mia starts hitting the target, the model, through multiple iterations and feedback, starts making accurate predictions.

In supervised learning, like Mia's training, the model learns from labeled examples, iteratively adjusting based on the feedback (error) until it can predict the outcomes reliably.

6.3 STORY: "THE ART TEACHER AND HER APPRENTICE"

IN a quaint town named DataVille, there was a renowned art teacher named Ms. Ada. She was famous for her impeccable artistry and had an apprentice, Leo, who was eager to learn. Leo was particularly fond of painting birds but struggled with capturing their true essence on canvas.

Seeing his enthusiasm, Ms. Ada decided to help him. She placed a beautiful picture of a sparrow on an easel and handed Leo a brush. "Now, watch closely," she said, as she began painting an exact replica of the sparrow beside the picture. With each brushstroke, she explained her choices of colors, techniques, and the reasons behind them.

As days turned into weeks, she would show him more pictures of various birds and guide him as he painted. Every time Leo

Figure 6.3: Prompt: A young painter painting an sparrow in oil and canvas style

made a mistake, Ms. Ada would gently correct him, ensuring he understood where he went wrong.

After several months of closely guided training, Leo was handed a picture of a bird he had never seen before—a magnificent kingfisher. Using what he had learned from Ms. Ada, he painted the bird beautifully. The town was in awe of his transformation. Leo had not just learned to paint a sparrow; under Ms. Ada's guidance, he'd learned to paint any bird.

ANALOGY EXPLANATION

In the story: - *Ms. Ada* represents the *algorithm* in supervised learning.

- *Leo* is the *model* being trained.

- The *pictures of birds* symbolize the *data with labels.* Each bird image (input) has a name or type (label).

- The process of Ms. Ada teaching Leo how to paint various birds based on the pictures is akin to how, in supervised learning, a model is trained on labeled data. The model learns the relationship between the inputs (features) and the desired output (label).

- When Leo successfully painted the kingfisher without direct guidance, it demonstrated the model's ability to *generalize* from its training to new, unseen data.

In essence, supervised learning is like having an expert teacher guide a student through examples until the student can perform on their own.

6.4   EXPLANATION AT THREE LEVELS OF DEPTH

The following descriptions explain "Supervised Learning" we explain this at three levels of depth.

SIMPLIFIED

Imagine you're learning to identify different fruits. The teacher shows you a picture of an apple and says, "This is an apple." Then she shows a banana and says, "This is a banana." After showing many fruits and naming them, she tests you with a new picture. Because you remember what she taught you, you can now tell it's an orange! Supervised learning is like this. Computers learn from examples given to them and then use that knowledge for new things.

GENERAL

Supervised learning is like studying with a guidebook that has questions and answers. Let's say you're prepping for a biology test. You review different questions with their correct answers (like "What's the powerhouse of the cell?" Answer: "Mitochondria"). After enough studying, when you see a new question on the test about cells, you can often guess the answer because of what you've studied. Similarly, in supervised learning, a computer is given data (questions) with known answers (labels). After "studying" enough, it can make educated guesses for new, similar data.

DETAILED

Supervised learning, a cornerstone of machine learning, involves training a model using a labeled dataset. In this paradigm, both input data (features) and the corresponding desired output (labels) are provided to the model during the training process. An algorithm iteratively adjusts the model by minimizing the difference between its predictions and the actual labels. The ultimate goal is for the model to generalize and make accurate predictions on new, unseen data. Popular methods in supervised learning include regression (for continuous outputs) and classification (for discrete outputs). The quality of the model is often evaluated using metrics like Mean Squared Error for regression tasks or accuracy for classification tasks.

CHAPTER 7

SUPERVISED LEARNING ALGORITHMS (LINEAR REGRESSION, LOGISTIC REGRESSION, DECISION TREES, SUPPORT VECTOR MACHINES AND K-NEAREST NEIGHBORS)

In the next three stories, we dive into 'Supervised Learning Algorithms, including Linear Regression, Logistic Regression, Decision Trees, Support Vector Machines, and K-Nearest Neighbors.' After each tale, we unpack the hidden analogies. We then offer simple, clear explanations designed to gradually enhance the reader's comprehension.

7.1 STORY: "THE GUARDIANS OF PREDICTA ISLAND"

IN the heart of the digital ocean lies Predicta Island, a place known for its ability to foresee the future. The island is protected by five guardian spirits, each possessing unique foresight skills.

1. *Linear Larry*, the first guardian, sees the world in lines. When villagers wish to predict how much rain they'd get based on cloud patterns, Larry draws a straight line through a cloud chart, guiding the villagers to understand the relationship between cloud formations and rain.

2. *Logistic Lucy*, the second guardian, was gifted with the power of choice. When the islanders are unsure whether to carry an umbrella (rain or no rain) or wear sunblock (sunny or not), Lucy takes into account several signs from nature and gives a "yes" or "no" answer.

3. *Dexter the Decision Tree* stands tall at the island's central square. He's like a magical flowchart. When someone asks a complicated question, like "Will this fruit tree bear fruit?", Dexter asks a series of yes-or-no questions, like "Did it rain last week?" or "Is the soil fertile?", guiding the islander to an answer.

4. *Valiant Vector*, the fourth guardian, is known for finding the best boundaries. Whenever two tribes have a dispute over land, Vector creates a clear, optimal boundary line (sometimes straight, sometimes curved) that ensures peace and balance between them.

5. *Kenny the Neighborly Spirit* doesn't predict on his own. Instead, he asks the closest spirits to him about their predictions. For instance, if an islander wants to know the best fishing spot, Kenny consults the nearest fishermen's spirits and directs the islander based on their collective wisdom.

Figure 7.1: Prompt: An sunny island with beautiful beaches has five armed five guardians on a beach in oil and canvas style

ANALOGY EXPLANATION

- *Linear Regression (Linear Larry)*: Like drawing a line to predict rain, linear regression finds the best straight line (linear relationship) that predicts the output based on one or more input variables.

- *Logistic Regression (Logistic Lucy)*: Used for binary classification tasks, it predicts the probability of an instance belonging to a default class, which can be converted into a "yes" or "no" decision.

- *Decision Trees (Dexter)*: A decision tree algorithm asks a series of questions and follows the answers (like a flowchart) to arrive at a decision.

- *Support Vector Machines (Valiant Vector)*: SVMs find the best boundary (or hyperplane) that best separates classes in a dataset. The boundary could be a line, curve, or more complex shape, depending on the data.

- *K-Nearest Neighbors (Kenny)*: KNN works by comparing a new data point to existing data points in the dataset. It then predicts the label based on the 'k' number of nearest neighbors.

7.2   STORY: "THE KINGDOM OF ALGORIA'S TALENT SHOW"

IN the magical kingdom of Algoria, King Datus announced a grand talent show. Five participants, each representing a unique skill, entered the stage.

1. *Linear the Predictor* had a vast scroll of the kingdom's history. When given any year, he'd draw a straight line on his scroll and predict the kingdom's wheat production. His predictions were continuous, like saying "5.2 tons" or "6.7 tons."

2. *Logan the Classifier* had a different scroll, but it was divided into two sections: Peace and War. People would give him a year, and Logan would place a marker on either 'Peace' or 'War',

predicting whether that year was peaceful or tumultuous based on past patterns.

3. *Treea the Decision-Maker* had a beautifully illustrated tree-shaped board. She'd ask questions starting from the top, like "Was it rainy?" and based on the answer, move to the next branch, finally making a prediction about a given situation at the bottom.

4. *Vectoria the Divider* brought a vast map of Algoria and several colored ropes. She placed towns (represented by pins) on the map and stretched ropes to ensure maximum distance between different types of towns. Her ropes determined the borders of regions, ensuring they were clearly distinguished.

5. *Neighborly Knox* had a simple pocket compass. He would find the 'k' nearest landmarks around a given point and then decide its nature. If 3 out of 5 closest landmarks were lakes, he'd predict the point to be water-based.

At the end of the talent show, King Datus realized that while each had their strengths, combining their talents could benefit the entire kingdom in various situations.

ANALOGY EXPLANATION

1. *Linear the Predictor (Linear Regression)*: Predicts a continuous output based on the relationship between input and output variables. The straight line represents the linear relationship.

2. *Logan the Classifier (Logistic Regression)*: Used for binary classification tasks (two outcomes). The 'Peace' or 'War' decision is binary.

3. *Treea the Decision-Maker (Decision Trees)*: Makes decisions based on asking a series of questions, represented by the branches of the tree.

4. *Vectoria the Divider (Support Vector Machines)*: Works by finding the hyperplane (represented by ropes) that best divides a dataset into classes.

Figure 7.2: Prompt: A talent show with five participants in oil and canvas style

5. *Neighborly Knox (K-Nearest Neighbors)*: Classifies data points based on how their neighbors are classified. The 'k' landmarks represent the k-nearest data points used for prediction.

7.3   STORY: "THE GREAT DATAVILLE COMPETITION"

ONCE upon a time in DataVille, the town council announced a competition to solve some of the town's most pressing challenges. Five unique and talented individuals stepped up, each with their own special approach to problem-solving.

1. *Larry the Line Drawer* had a straightforward approach. Given a challenge, Larry would lay out all the data points on a big board and draw a straight line that best captured the general trend. For instance, when asked about predicting the price of houses based on their size, Larry's line showed that as size increased, so did the price.

2. *Lola the Logistician* had a peculiar way of dividing things into two. She'd look at data and say, "This belongs here or there." When the town wanted to know if a house with certain features would be bought quickly or not, Lola confidently sorted them into "Fast Sale" or "Slow Sale".

3. *Danny the Decision-Maker* had a vast book of rules. He'd ask a series of yes-or-no questions until he pinpointed an answer. To determine what activity a townsperson might enjoy, he'd ask: "Do they like outdoors? If yes, do they prefer water or mountains?" And so on, until he'd suggest "They'd love kayaking!" or "They'd enjoy hiking!".

4. *Sylvia the Separator* had an elegant technique. She'd place all data on a vast plane and magically find the best boundary that separated different groups, ensuring that similar items stayed together, but apart from different ones.

Figure 7.3: Prompt: A competition to solve problems of a town and its five competitors in oil and canvas style

5. *Kevin, Keeper of Neighbors*, always believed in community. Whenever given a challenge, Kevin would look at the closest examples he knew of and decide based on the majority. "This new song," he'd muse, "sounds like 5 others I know, and 4 of those were hits. It'll probably be a hit!"

The competition revealed that no single approach was the best for all problems. Each had its strengths, and the best method often depended on the specific challenge.

ANALOGY EXPLANATION

1. *Larry the Line Drawer* represents *Linear Regression*. He draws the best fit line through data, typically used for continuous predictions like house prices based on size.

2. *Lola the Logistician* symbolizes *Logistic Regression*. Her binary choices reflect the algorithm's knack for binary classification problems, such as categorizing houses by sale speed.

3. *Danny the Decision-Maker* is analogous to *Decision Trees*. His structured rule-based questions mirror how decision trees split data based on features.

4. *Sylvia the Separator* stands for *Support Vector Machines (SVM)*. Her ability to find the best boundary between data groups mirrors SVM's capacity to find hyperplanes that best separate different classes.

5. *Kevin, Keeper of Neighbors* embodies the *k-Nearest Neighbors (k-NN)* algorithm. His method of basing decisions on the closest known examples reflects k-NN's approach of classifying based on the proximity of data points.

7.4 EXPLANATION AT THREE LEVELS OF DEPTH

The following descriptions explain "Supervised Learning Algorithms; Linear Regression, Logistic Regression, Decision Trees, Support Vector Machines and K-Nearest Neighbors" at three levels of depth.

SIMPLIFIED

- **Linear Regression:** Imagine you're drawing a straight line through a group of scattered stickers on a wall. This line tries to be as close as possible to all the stickers.

- **Logistic Regression:** Think of it as a light switch, either ON or OFF. Based on things you know, you decide whether to turn a light ON (yes) or OFF (no).

- **Decision Trees:** It's like playing a game of "20 Questions." You ask questions to guess something, and each answer guides your next question until you find the answer.

- **Support Vector Machines:** Imagine a boy or a girl is arranging toy cars and dolls on a playmat. You try to draw a line (or put a string) that best separates the two groups, ensuring they don't mix.

- **K-Nearest Neighbors:** Say they found a toy but didn't know if it belonged to the dolls or cars group. They'd see where they found it and which toys are closest to decide where it belongs.

GENERAL

- **Linear Regression:** This is a statistical method to predict a value (like a student's final grade) based on one or more other values (like midterm grades and attendance).

- **Logistic Regression:** Used for classification. For example, it can predict whether a student will pass (1) or fail (0) based on study hours, attendance, etc.

- **Decision Trees:** This algorithm sorts data by asking a series of questions. For instance, to predict if someone might like a movie, it could ask: "Is it action? If yes, does it have the student's favorite actor?"

- **Support Vector Machines:** SVM finds the best boundary (or line in 2D, plane in 3D) that separates different categories of data.

- **K-Nearest Neighbors:** If you're classifying a data point, you'd look at the 'k' number of closest points (or neighbors) to it and see which category most of those neighbors belong to. That's your answer.

Detailed

- **Linear Regression:** It's a linear approach to modeling the relationship between a scalar dependent variable and one or more independent variables by fitting a linear equation to observed data.

- **Logistic Regression:** Despite its name, logistic regression is used for binary classification. It estimates the parameters of a logistic model, making the outcome between 0 and 1.

- **Decision Trees:** A flowchart-like structure where each internal node represents a feature(or attribute), each leaf node represents a decision (or class label), and branches represent conjunctions of features leading to those decisions.

- **Support Vector Machines:** A supervised ML model which seeks to find the optimal hyperplane that maximizes the margin between two classes in a dataset. This margin is defined by support vectors.

- **K-Nearest Neighbors:** A non-parametric, lazy learning algorithm that classifies a data point based on how its neighbors are classified. It stores instances of the training dataset and uses a distance metric to find the 'k' nearest points, which then vote on classification.

CHAPTER 8

REGRESSION & CLASSIFICATION

In our next three stories, we delve into 'Regression and Classification within Supervised Learning.' After each narrative, we decipher the underlying analogies. Then, we provide lucid explanations at three levels of detail guiding readers toward a progressively richer understanding.

8.1 STORY: "THE MAGICAL MARKET OF PREDICTA"

IN the enchanted town of Predicta, there was a unique market known far and wide. The market had two famous stalls: "The Weight Whisperer" and "The Color Classifier."

The Weight Whisperer was run by an old sage named Remy. People from all over came to him with fruits of unknown weight. They would describe the fruit's size, shape, and other details. Using his magical scales, Remy would predict the exact weight of the fruit. One day, a farmer described a gigantic apple he had grown, and Remy estimated it to be around 250 grams.

Beside Remy's stall was *The Color Classifier* managed by a young enchantress named Clara. Clara had a peculiar talent: she could classify anything into categories based on descriptions. People would describe objects to her, and she would instantly tell them its color. A traveler once described a feather he found on his journey, and Clara immediately proclaimed it to be from a blue bird.

Both Remy and Clara had their magic, but while Remy's predictions were about numbers (like the weight of fruits), Clara's magic sorted things into clear groups (like colors).

ANALOGY EXPLANATION

- *The Weight Whisperer (Remy)*: This stall represents *regression* in supervised learning. Just as Remy predicts a continuous value (the weight of the fruit) based on its description, regression models predict a continuous outcome based on input features.

- *The Color Classifier (Clara)*: Clara's stall is an analogy for *classification* in supervised learning. Classification is about categorizing data points. When Clara hears a description, she categorizes the item into a particular class (like identifying the color of an object). Similarly, classification models in machine learning categorize input data into distinct labels or classes.

In essence, while both stalls in the market of Predicta use descriptions to make predictions, Remy's stall predicts quantities, and Clara's stall categorizes things into groups.

8.2   STORY: "THE MAGIC ORCHARD OF PREDICTIONS"

IN the enchanting land of Algorithmia, there was a mystical orchard known to the locals as the Magic Orchard of

Figure 8.1: Prompt: Two people, one male and the other is female, thinking hard to make a good guess in oil and canvas style

Predictions. This orchard was unique for it bore two distinct types of fruits - the Crystal Apples and the Sorting Pears.

Crystal Apples:

Whenever a villager found themselves uncertain about a numerical question, such as "How many sheep will I have next year?" or "What will be the height of my corn plants?", they would visit the orchard and pick a Crystal Apple. They'd whisper their question to the apple, and magically, the apple would fill with swirling numbers, eventually settling on one clear number, providing the answer.

Sorting Pears:

For questions related to categories, like "Will this seed grow into a blue or red flower?" or "Is this a safe herb or a poisonous one?", villagers would pick a Sorting Pear. After the question was whispered, the pear would either turn the color of the flower in question or display a symbol representing safety or danger.

Over time, the orchard became an essential part of the village. While the young ones believed it was pure magic, the elders knew that the orchard's magic was the wisdom of generations before them, who had observed patterns and passed them on.

ANALOGY EXPLANATION

In the story:

- The *Magic Orchard* represents the world of *supervised learning*.

- *Crystal Apples* symbolize *regression* tasks in machine learning. Just as the apples provide a numerical answer (like the height of a plant or number of sheep), regression models in machine learning predict a continuous value or quantity based on input data.

- *Sorting Pears* stand for *classification* tasks. Like the pears that categorize answers (blue/red flower or safe/poisonous herb), classification models in supervised learning categorize input data into specific classes or labels based on its features.

Figure 8.2: Prompt: A magic orchard in the style of digital art

Together, the fruits of the Magic Orchard demonstrate the two fundamental approaches of supervised learning, showing how data can be used either to predict a value or classify into categories.

8.3 STORY: "THE MYSTIC SEER OF DATAVILLE"

IN the vibrant town of DataVille, there lived a mystic seer named Clara. Clara possessed a unique crystal ball, which the townsfolk believed had two incredible abilities: predicting the exact height of a child when they'd grow up and identifying the jobs they'd take on as adults.

One day, a couple approached Clara with their young son, Timmy, curious about his future. Clara first placed a ruler beside the crystal ball and gazed deeply into it. "Timmy," she said, "will grow up to be exactly 6 feet 2 inches tall." The couple jotted down the prediction, amazed by the seer's precision.

Next, Clara shuffled a deck of cards, each bearing a different profession: baker, blacksmith, knight, and so on. She placed a card on the crystal ball and waited. After a moment, an image of Timmy wearing a crown appeared. "He will become the king of DataVille!" Clara exclaimed.

Over the years, many parents visited Clara. And as the children grew, the townsfolk noticed that while she sometimes didn't get the exact height right, she was always in the ballpark. And as for the professions? Clara's predictions turned out to be uncannily accurate.

ANALOGY EXPLANATION

In this story:

- Clara's prediction of *Timmy's height* represents *regression* in supervised learning. Regression deals with predicting a continuous

Figure 8.3: Prompt: A mystic seer looking into her crystal ball in the style of digital art

value. Just as Clara tried to predict the exact height Timmy would grow up to, regression models aim to predict a continuous output based on given input(s).

- The prediction of *Timmy's future profession* using the deck of cards symbolizes *classification* in supervised learning. Classification is about categorizing data into predefined classes or labels. Clara's use of the profession cards to determine which job Timmy would take on is analogous to a classification task, where models predict which category (or class) an input belongs to.

In the context of supervised learning, both regression and classification rely on labeled examples to train, but the nature of the prediction (continuous vs. categorical) differentiates the two.

8.4 Explanation at Three Levels of Depth

The following descriptions explain "Regression & Classification" at three increasing levels of depth.

Simplified

Imagine you have a magic box. If you show it a photo of a baby animal and ask, "How big will it get?", the box will tell you its size when it's all grown up. That's like **regression** – guessing a number, like height or weight. Now, if you ask the box, "What kind of animal is this?", it might say "kitten" or "puppy." That's **classification** – putting things into groups or categories.

General

Think of supervised learning as a teacher training you for a quiz. For **regression**, it's like guessing the weight of a bag of candies. You're trying to predict a number. For example, if you're given data about a car's speed and you have to predict how long it'll take to stop, that's regression.

Classification, on the other hand, is like sorting those candies by flavor. You're not predicting a number but a category. So, if you're given a person's shopping habits and you have to guess if they'd prefer chocolate or vanilla, that's classification.

DETAILED

In the realm of supervised machine learning, both regression and classification are cornerstone techniques.

Regression involves predicting a continuous target variable based on one or multiple input features. The primary goal is to model and understand the relationships between inputs and outputs. Examples include predicting stock prices, estimating house values, or forecasting sales. Common algorithms include linear regression, ridge regression, and support vector regression.

Classification, in contrast, deals with predicting discrete categories or classes for given inputs. The aim is to assign new input data to one of the known categories based on its features. Use cases range from medical diagnoses (e.g., classifying tumors as benign or malignant) to image recognition (e.g., identifying handwritten digits). Familiar classification algorithms include logistic regression, decision trees, and neural networks.

Both methodologies use labeled datasets for training, optimizing model parameters to minimize prediction errors, but the nature of their output (continuous vs. categorical) distinguishes them.

CHAPTER 9

EVALUATION METRICS
FOR CLASSIFICATION

In our next three tales, we dive into the 'Evaluation Metrics for Classification.' Following each narrative, we unpack the woven-in analogies. We then offer concise explanations for readers at three levels of detail, enabling them to gradually enhance their comprehension.

9.1 STORY: "THE TALE OF THE GOLDEN COOKIE CONTEST"

IN the town of Byteville, the annual Golden Cookie Contest was a cherished tradition. Bakers would present their cookies, and judges had to classify each cookie as either "Golden" (the highest quality) or "Regular."

Miss Ada, a renowned baker, had designed a machine to help her predict the quality of cookies. Eager to test its performance, she fed the machine a batch of cookies she already knew the classification for.

1. When a cookie was truly of "Golden" quality and the machine predicted it as "Golden," it earned a "Golden Star."

2. But if a cookie was just "Regular" and the machine wrongly predicted it as "Golden," it was tagged with a "Fool's Gold" label.

3. If a "Golden" cookie was misclassified as "Regular," it was marked as a "Lost Treasure."

4. And when a "Regular" cookie was correctly identified as "Regular," it was given a "True Tale" badge.

To gauge her machine's accuracy: - Miss Ada measured *Accuracy* by dividing the sum of "Golden Stars" and "True Tales" by the total number of cookies.

- The *Precision* for Golden cookies was found by dividing "Golden Stars" by the sum of "Golden Stars" and "Fool's Gold."

- *Recall* for Golden cookies was the "Golden Stars" divided by the sum of "Golden Stars" and "Lost Treasures."

- To get an overall sense of the balance between Precision and Recall, she calculated the *F1 Score*.

- Lastly, she drew a *ROC Curve* to understand the trade-off between correctly predicting "Golden" cookies and mistakenly predicting "Regular" ones as "Golden."

At the end of her experiment, Miss Ada not only had a clearer picture of her machine's predictions but also of the intricacies of classification metrics.

ANALOGY EXPLANATION

1. *Golden Star* represents *True Positives (TP)*: Correctly predicted positive cases.

2. *Fool's Gold* corresponds to *False Positives (FP)*: Negative cases incorrectly predicted as positive.

3. *Lost Treasure* stands for *False Negatives (FN)*: Positive cases incorrectly predicted as negative.

4. *True Tale* is equivalent to *True Negatives (TN)*: Correctly predicted negative cases.

Figure 9.1: Prompt: Judges tasting cookies in the Golden Cookie Contest in the style of digital art

- *Accuracy*: It gives a general measure of how often the classifier is correct. Formula: (TP + TN) / (TP + FP + FN + TN)

- *Precision*: Indicates how many of the predicted positive cases were actually positive. Formula: TP / (TP + FP)

- *Recall or Sensitivity*: It tells how many of the actual positive cases were caught. Formula: TP / (TP + FN) - *F1 Score*: Harmonic mean of Precision and Recall. It provides a balance between the two. Formula: 2 * (Precision * Recall) / (Precision + Recall)

- *ROC Curve (Receiver Operating Characteristic)*: It plots the True Positive Rate (Recall) against the False Positive Rate. The area under this curve (AUC) provides a measure of the model's performance across all classification thresholds.

9.2 STORY: "THE MYSTERY OF THE MAGIC AMULETS"

In the mystical land of Algora, there were two kinds of amulets – the true Magic Amulets, which brought good fortune, and the mundane ones, which were just ornamental. Sir Eval, a knight, was tasked with identifying the real Magic Amulets using a special machine he had developed.

1. Every time the machine identified an amulet as magical and it truly was, a bell in the town square rang, signaling a *True Magic Moment*.

2. Sometimes, the machine thought an ordinary amulet was magical. This led to a *False Magic Alarm*.

3. In rare moments, the machine missed recognizing a real Magic Amulet, marking a *Magic Missed Moment*.

4. And when an ordinary amulet was correctly identified as such, the townsfolk celebrated the *Realistic Recognition*.

At the end of the day, Sir Eval sat down to gauge his machine's performance:

- He calculated *Accuracy* by checking how often the machine was right, counting both the True Magic Moments and the Realistic Recognitions.

- *Precision* was the number of True Magic Moments divided by all moments when the machine believed it found magic, including the False Magic Alarms.

- To measure *Recall*, Sir Eval considered how many True Magic Moments there were out of all potential magical moments, including those that were missed.

- Realizing that both Precision and Recall were vital, he combined them to compute the *F1 Score*.

- Finally, as he adjusted the machine's sensitivity, he plotted its True Magic detection rate against its False Magic rate, drawing the enigmatic *ROC Curve*.

When he presented his results, the townsfolk not only appreciated the machine's capabilities but also understood the challenges of classification.

ANALOGY EXPLANATION

1. *True Magic Moment* represents *True Positives (TP)*: Actual positives correctly identified.

2. *False Magic Alarm* stands for *False Positives (FP)*: Actual negatives wrongly identified as positives.

3. *Magic Missed Moment* corresponds to *False Negatives (FN)*: Actual positives that were missed.

4. *Realistic Recognition* is akin to *True Negatives (TN)*: Actual negatives correctly identified.

- *Accuracy*: Gives an overall measure of the classifier's performance. Formula: (TP + TN) / (TP + FP + FN + TN)

- *Precision*: Reflects how many of the identified positives are actually positive. Formula: TP / (TP + FP)

- *Recall*: Shows the proportion of actual positives that were identified. Formula: TP / (TP + FN)

Figure 9.2: Prompt: Shinny colorful magic amulets and ordinary ornaments in digital art style.

- *F1 Score*: The harmonic mean of Precision and Recall, balancing the two. Formula: 2 * (Precision * Recall) / (Precision + Recall)

- *ROC Curve (Receiver Operating Characteristic)*: Plots the True Positive Rate against the False Positive Rate, showing the trade-offs at various thresholds.

9.3   STORY: "THE GREAT FRUIT SORTING FESTIVAL"

IN the village of Dataville, the Great Fruit Sorting Festival was an event everyone looked forward to. Every year, children would try to sort apples from oranges. Little Alice, always the tinkerer, built a machine for the job.

She tested her machine with a basket full of fruits she already knew were apples or oranges.

1. Whenever the machine correctly identified an apple, the villagers cheered, "Bullseye!"

2. If it mistook an orange for an apple, there was a humorous, "Oops-a-daisy!"

3. When an apple was wrongly declared as an orange, kids would sigh, "Missed it!"

4. Correctly spotting an orange led to a calm nod and a comment, "As expected."

Alice wanted to know just how good her machine was:

- She tallied the cheers to calculate *Accuracy* by taking the sum of "Bullseye!" and "As expected." moments and dividing it by the total fruits.

- *Precision* for apples was counted as the "Bullseye!" shouts divided by all occasions the machine declared something as an apple (sum of "Bullseye!" and "Oops-a-daisy!").

- To measure *Recall* for apples, Alice divided the "Bullseye!" events by the times the machine should have identified an apple (sum of "Bullseye!" and "Missed it!").

- Combining Precision and Recall, Alice used the *F1 Score* as an overall performance grade.

- Additionally, Alice drew a curve for every time the machine was more confident about sorting, calling it the *ROC Curve*. The area beneath this curve, the village elder told her, showed the machine's ability to distinguish between the fruits clearly.

By festival's end, Alice not only knew how effective her machine was but also learned the importance of each metric in machine evaluation.

ANALOGY EXPLANATION

1. *Bullseye!* corresponds to *True Positives (TP)*: Correctly predicted positive cases (apples).

2. *Oops-a-daisy!* symbolizes *False Positives (FP)*: Negative cases (oranges) wrongly predicted as positive (apples).

3. *Missed it!* stands for *False Negatives (FN)*: Positive cases (apples) wrongly predicted as negative (oranges).

4. *As expected.* is equivalent to *True Negatives (TN)*: Correctly predicted negative cases (oranges).

- *Accuracy*: Gives an overall measure of the classifier's correctness. Formula: (TP + TN) / (TP + FP + FN + TN).

- *Precision*: Indicates how often the machine's apple predictions were correct. Formula: TP / (TP + FP).

- *Recall or Sensitivity*: Tells the proportion of actual apples correctly identified. Formula: TP / (TP + FN).

- *F1 Score*: Harmonic mean of Precision and Recall. Balances both metrics. Formula: 2 * (Precision * Recall) / (Precision + Recall).

Figure 9.3: Prompt: A machine sorts oranges and apples in an orchard in digital art style

- *ROC Curve (Receiver Operating Characteristic)*: Plots the True Positive Rate against the False Positive Rate. The area under this curve (AUC) is a measure of the model's overall performance.

9.4 EXPLANATION AT THREE LEVELS OF DEPTH

The following descriptions explain "Evaluation metrics for classification in supervised learning" at three levels of complexity.

SIMPLIFIED

Imagine there is a magic box that can guess if a toy is a car or a doll. You test it to see how good it is:

- **Accuracy**: It's like checking how many toys the box guessed right out of all the toys you showed it. If it gets 8 out of 10 toys right, its accuracy is 80

- **Precision**: Suppose you only look at the cars. If the box says "this is a car" 5 times but is only correct 4 times, then its precision is 4 out of 5, or 80%. It's like checking how often the box is right when it says "car".

- **Recall**: Now, think of the 7 cars you have. If the box correctly spots 4 of them as cars, then its recall is 4 out of 7. It's like seeing how many cars the box can find from all the cars you have.

- **F1 Score**: Imagine taking precision and recall and combining them into a single score to see overall how the box is doing.

- **ROC Curve**: This is a bit tricky. Let's say your box is not just saying "car" or "doll", but is also saying how sure it is. So, sometimes it might be very sure it's a car, other times, not so much. ROC Curve helps us see how good the box is when it's very sure and when it's a little sure.

GENERAL

In machine learning, we create models to classify things. When testing these models, we look at several metrics:

- **Accuracy**: It's the ratio of correct predictions to total predictions. If a model correctly predicts 80 out of 100 samples, its accuracy is 80

- **Precision**: Out of all the positive predictions made, how many were actually correct? It's calculated as True Positives / (True Positives + False Positives).

- **Recall or Sensitivity**: Out of all the actual positive cases, how many did we predict correctly? It's True Positives / (True Positives + False Negatives).

- **F1 Score**: It's the harmonic mean of precision and recall, providing a balanced measure.

- **ROC Curve**: It's a graph that shows the performance of a classification model at different thresholds, plotting the True Positive Rate against the False Positive Rate. The better the model, the more the curve bows towards the top left.

DETAILED

Evaluation metrics are fundamental in gauging the efficacy of a classification model, both in binary and multi-class scenarios:

- **Accuracy**: It's a primary metric calculated as (TP + TN) / (TP + TN + FP + FN). However, it can be misleading, especially in imbalanced datasets.

- **Precision**: Precision provides an indication of the model's positive predictive power. It's the ratio of correctly predicted positive observations to the total predicted positives.

- **Recall or Sensitivity**: This metric showcases the model's capability to find all the applicable data points. It's vital in scenarios where False Negatives are particularly costly.

- **F1 Score**: Being the harmonic mean of precision and recall, F1 score is particularly useful when class distribution is uneven.

- **ROC Curve and AUC**: The ROC Curve provides a comprehensive view of model performance across varying thresholds, with AUC quantifying the overall skill of the model. An AUC of 1 denotes a perfect classifier, while an AUC of 0.5 indicates no discrimination capability.

These metrics, when combined, offer a holistic view of the model's performance and are indispensable in fine-tuning and model selection.

CHAPTER 10

EVALUATION METRICS FOR REGRESSION

In the upcoming trio of stories, we delve into the 'Evaluation Metrics for Regression.' After each tale, we decode the integrated analogies. Subsequently, we provide succinct explanations at three levels of detail helping readers to gradually enhance their understanding.

10.1 STORY: "THE GREAT ARCHER'S AIM"

In a tranquil village nestled between lush forests and rolling hills, a yearly event drew crowds from all corners – The Great Archer's Tournament. Competing archers would aim at targets set at varying distances, and the one with the most consistent and accurate shots would be crowned the champion.

This year, a wise sage introduced new methods to measure each archer's prowess:

1. *The Gentle Tug (Mean Absolute Error - MAE)*

After each shot, children would measure the distance between the arrow and the bullseye using a soft rope. They would then take an average of all these distances across all arrows to determine how far, on average, the archer's shots were from perfection. If an archer's arrow landed right on the bullseye, the length of the rope would be zero!

2. *The Strong Pull (Mean Squared Error - MSE)*

A group of scholars, preferring to emphasize mistakes, suggested a different measure. For each arrow, they would square the distance to the bullseye. This made larger errors more pronounced than smaller ones. The average of these squared distances would then be taken. An almost perfect archer with one terrible shot might find themselves penalized heavily.

3. *The Mirror's Reflection (R-squared)*

At the end of the field was a magical mirror. It would show how much better an archer's shots were compared to someone shooting arrows randomly. If the mirror showed a full, clear image, it meant the archer's shots were perfect (R-squared = 1). But if it showed a foggy or fragmented reflection, it depicted that there wasn't much difference between the archer's skill and random shots.

4. *The Traveling Merchant's Gauge (Mean Absolute Percentage Error - MAPE)*

A traveling merchant suggested a relative measure. He would look at how far each arrow was from the bullseye and express it as a percentage of the bullseye's value. He'd then take an average of these percentages. This way, he could relate the error of an archer's shot to the perfection of the bullseye, giving everyone a sense of proportion.

ANALOGY EXPLANATION

- *The Gentle Tug (MAE)*: This measures the average "distance" from the bullseye, representing the average error. In real-

Figure 10.1: Prompt: A village nestled between forests and rolling hills in digital art style

world regression, it's the average absolute difference between the predicted and actual values.

- *The Strong Pull (MSE)*: By squaring the errors, larger mistakes are given more weight, which can be more penalizing for models that have occasional large errors.

- *The Mirror's Reflection (R-squared)*: It's a relative metric showing how much better our model is compared to a naive model. In our story, it compares the archer's skill to someone shooting arrows without aiming.

- *The Traveling Merchant's Gauge (MAPE)*: It provides a relative error measurement, showcasing errors as a percentage of the actual values (or the bullseye in the story), which can be helpful in contexts where relative error matters more than absolute error.

10.2 Story: "The Village of Preciseland"

IN the scenic village of Preciseland, they had an annual tradition. Every summer, villagers would gather at the main square to participate in the "Rock Toss Festival." The challenge was simple: toss a rock and try to get it as close to a marked golden spot on the ground.

1. *Mean Absolute Error (MAE)*: Young Billy always kept a tape measure handy. After each toss, he'd measure the straight-line distance between where his rock landed and the golden spot. He'd note down all the distances, regardless of whether the rock landed to the left or right of the spot. At the end of his turns, he'd average out these measurements. He explained, "I just want to know, on average, how far off my throws are."

2. *Mean Squared Error (MSE)*: Emily, a local schoolteacher, had a different approach. For every throw that wasn't spot-on, she felt a pang of disappointment. She squared her errors because she

believed mistakes should have weight. If she missed by a lot, the disappointment was significantly higher. "It's not just about how far we miss; it's about the weight of our mistakes," she'd muse.

3. *R-squared*: Old Man Jenkins, a village elder, sat on his porch overseeing the game. He was less interested in individual throws and more about the overall pattern. He would comment, "If most rocks land close to the golden spot and very few are way off, then it's a successful day for Preciseland." He was all about capturing the overall variance and consistency of throws.

4. *Mean Absolute Percentage Error (MAPE)*: Clarissa, the market trader, always had an eye for percentages. Instead of just looking at raw distances like Billy, she would calculate how much each throw was off as a percentage of how close it could've been to the golden spot. "Everything's about proportions and percentages in trading, and so is my game strategy," she'd explain.

ANALOGY EXPLANATION

- *MAE*: Just as Billy measured the direct distance from his rock to the golden spot, MAE measures the average of the absolute differences between predicted and actual values.

- *MSE*: Like Emily squaring her distances to give weight to larger mistakes, MSE squares the differences before averaging them, giving more weight to larger errors.

- *R-squared*: Old Man Jenkins' perspective reflects R-squared. It provides a measure of how well the observed outcomes are replicated by the model, based on the proportion of total variation of outcomes explained by the model.

- *MAPE*: Clarissa's percentage-based approach resonates with MAPE. It calculates the error as a percentage, providing a relative measure of accuracy.

Figure 10.2: Prompt: A festival in a scenic village in digital art style

10.3 STORY: "THE APPLE HARVEST CONTEST"

IN the orchard town of Numerica, there was an annual apple harvest contest. Farmers would guess how many apples their trees would produce. At the end of the season, they'd compare their predictions to the actual yield. Different neighbors had unique ways of seeing who was closest to their predictions.

1. *Mean Absolute Error (MAE)*: Little Sammy was straightforward. After the harvest, he'd take each tree, see how many apples off the prediction was made, and then find the average difference. For Sammy, whether you predicted 10 apples too many or 10 apples too few, it was still 10 apples off. His method was like taking the absolute value of each error and then averaging them.

2. *Mean Squared Error (MSE)*: Jenny, Sammy's neighbor, was stricter. She believed that bigger mistakes should be punished more. If a prediction was 10 apples off, she thought of it as 100 (10 squared) apples wrong, and if it was 20 apples off, it was like being 400 apples off! By squaring each error and then taking the average, she emphasized larger mistakes.

3. *R-squared*: Old Farmer Gray wasn't as concerned with individual errors. Instead, he looked at the overall picture. He'd often muse, "Well, if I just predicted the average apple yield every time, how much better is my current method?" He was comparing the variance captured by the actual predictions against a simple average model. This was the concept of R-squared, showing how much better the model's predictions were compared to just predicting the average.

4. *Mean Absolute Percentage Error (MAPE)*: Clara, a schoolteacher, approached it differently. She'd look at each prediction and calculate how many percent off it was from the

Figure 10.3: Prompt: An apple harvest contest in a scenic town in digital art style

actual count. "It gives me a sense of scale," she'd say, comparing errors relative to the size of the actual values.

ANALOGY EXPLANATION

- *MAE*: Like Sammy's simple method, MAE is all about the average absolute error. It doesn't matter if you overpredict or underpredict; it's about how much you're off on average.

- *MSE*: Just as Jenny emphasized bigger errors by squaring them, MSE does the same. Bigger mistakes are highlighted more in this metric, making it sensitive to outliers.

- *R-squared*: Farmer Gray's method mirrors R-squared. It gives a sense of how much our prediction model improves upon a naive model that just predicts the average outcome for every instance.

- *MAPE*: Clara's percentage approach is the essence of MAPE. It's about understanding errors in terms of their relative size to actual values. It provides a sense of scale, especially useful when actual values vary a lot in magnitude.

10.4 EXPLANATION AT THREE LEVELS OF DEPTH

The following descriptions explain "Evaluation Metrics for Regression in Supervised Learning" in three levels of detail.

SIMPLIFIED

Imagine you are trying to guess the number of candies in a jar. After you've made your guess, we need ways to check how close you were to the real number.

- **Mean Absolute Error (MAE)**: Let's say you guessed 10 candies too many in one jar and 10 too few in another. We just take the simple difference, like saying "I was off by 10 candies."

- **Mean Squared Error (MSE)**: Now, instead of just counting the difference, imagine squaring them. If you're off by a little, it's not a big deal, but if you're off by a lot, that mistake gets really big!

- **R-squared**: Suppose you always guessed there were 50 candies, no matter the jar size. How much better is your actual guess compared to always saying 50? That's what R-squared tells us!

- **Mean Absolute Percentage Error (MAPE)**: This is like asking, "What percentage off was my guess from the actual number of candies?"

GENERAL

When we try to predict something using a model, we want to see how well our model did.

- **Mean Absolute Error (MAE)**: This is the average of the absolute differences between our predictions and the actual values. It gives us a direct sense of the average size of the errors.

- **Mean Squared Error (MSE)**: Here, we square the differences between our predictions and the actual values and then take the average. It's sensitive to large errors since squaring emphasizes bigger differences.

- **R-squared**: It's a measure of how well our model's predictions match the actual data, compared to if we just predicted the average value every time. A value of 1 is perfect, and a value of 0 means our model is no better than just guessing the average.

- **Mean Absolute Percentage Error (MAPE)**: This metric gives the average percentage error between our predicted and actual values. It's particularly useful when we want to understand the error relative to the size of the things we're predicting.

DETAILED

In regression analysis, evaluating the precision and reliability of model predictions is crucial.

- **Mean Absolute Error (MAE)**: It provides a linear penalty for each unit of difference between the predicted and observed values. It's computationally simple and easy to interpret.

- **Mean Squared Error (MSE)**: By squaring the residuals, MSE gives higher weight to larger errors. This can be advantageous when larger errors are particularly undesirable, but it can be sensitive to outliers.

- **R-squared**: Also known as the coefficient of determination, it quantifies the proportion of variance in the dependent variable that is predictable from the independent variables. It offers insight into the goodness-of-fit of the model.

- **Mean Absolute Percentage Error (MAPE)**: It scales the absolute error as a percentage of the actual value. This is particularly useful when dealing with values of varied magnitudes, providing a relative measure of error across datasets. However, it's undefined for zero actual values and can be overly sensitive for values close to zero.

Chapter 11

Unsupervised Learning

In the following three tales, we journey through unsupervised learning. After each narrative, we decode the interwoven analogies. Then, we present straightforward explanations at three levels of detail to progressively enhance the understanding of the reader.

11.1 Story: "The Mystery Island and the Treasure Clusters"

ON a bright summer day, young explorers Mike and Emma discovered a mystery island. They heard legends that the island held numerous hidden treasures scattered across its expanse. Excited by the potential adventure, they set out to find as many treasures as they could.

But there was a catch: the map they had didn't show the exact locations of the treasures. Instead, it contained cryptic symbols and patterns. Without specific locations, they decided to search the island and mark places where they found similar kinds of treasures.

After days of exploration, they noticed certain patterns:

1. The northern part of the island had mostly ancient coins.

2. The eastern side had colorful gemstones.

Figure 11.1: Prompt: Map of a treasure island in digital art style.

3. The western region had old, mysterious scrolls.

4. The southern beaches had rare shells.

Mike and Emma realized that even without a precise map, they could find treasures by understanding these patterns and clusters. Instead of searching the entire island blindly, they focused on specific areas depending on the type of treasure they were interested in. By the end of their adventure, they had a rich collection of diverse treasures.

ANALOGY EXPLANATION

In the story, the island represents a dataset. The treasures scattered on the island represent data points in this dataset.

The catch is that Mike and Emma didn't have labels or exact locations for where each treasure would be (much like how in unsupervised learning, we don't have predefined labels).

However, as they explored, they began to notice patterns and clusters of similar kinds of treasures. This clustering is analogous to unsupervised learning techniques where the algorithm identifies structures or patterns in the data on its own, grouping data points with similar characteristics.

Their realization and subsequent strategy to focus on specific regions based on the type of treasure is similar to how unsupervised learning can help in understanding hidden structures in data and can aid in more targeted explorations or decision-making.

11.2 STORY: "THE MYSTERIOUS ISLAND OF TOYS"

IN a faraway land, there was a mysterious island where toys from all over the world ended up when they were lost or forgotten. One day, Ellie, a curious young girl, found herself on this island. She was amazed by the variety of toys: dolls, cars, blocks, stuffed animals, and more. They were all mixed together without any order.

Ellie decided to help the toys find their groups. She didn't know the names or exact types of these toys, nor did anyone tell her how to classify them. However, she started observing patterns. She noticed that all the toys with wheels often moved around, so she put them in one corner. The toys that were soft and cuddly,

Figure 11.2: Prompt: A shore with many toys in digital art style

she placed in another area. Toys that had pieces fitting together, like puzzles and blocks, went into another group.

Over time, Ellie had managed to form distinct groups of toys, based solely on their similarities and differences, without any prior knowledge about them.

ANALOGY EXPLANATION

In this story, the island represents a dataset with numerous data points (toys). Ellie's task of grouping the toys without prior labels or instructions represents *unsupervised learning*.

- *Toys on the Island*: These symbolize the data in our dataset. They come in different shapes, sizes, and features but lack explicit labels.

- *Ellie's Observations*: Ellie's method of grouping toys based on their inherent features is analogous to how unsupervised learning algorithms work. They identify patterns and structures in the data without being explicitly told what to look for.

- *The Formed Groups*: These are the clusters or groupings created by unsupervised learning algorithms, like clusters in clustering algorithms.

This story illustrates that, in unsupervised learning, the algorithm works without prior guidance, finding hidden patterns and structures in data, much like Ellie did on the mysterious island of toys.

11.3 STORY: "THE MAGICAL GIFT TREE"

ON a remote island, there was a peculiar event every year. A magical tree, known as the "Gifting Tree," would drop hundreds of toys. These toys weren't labeled, categorized, or named; they just existed in a beautiful array of shapes, sizes, and colors.

The island had never seen outsiders before, but one day, a young explorer named Mia arrived. Mia noticed the scattered toys and thought it would be a great idea to organize them. Without any prior knowledge about the toys or their names, she decided to group them based solely on their similarities.

She placed toys that looked like vehicles - cars, trucks, planes - in one area. Toys that looked like animals, regardless of their size, went into another group. Building blocks, due to their similar shapes and functionalities, formed another cluster. And so, Mia

Figure 11.3: Prompt: A magical gift tree dropping toys in digital art style

continued, creating groups solely based on the inherent features of the toys.

At the end of her task, the island's inhabitants were amazed. They could now easily find toys of a certain type, even if they didn't know its name or purpose. Mia's intuitive grouping system became the new way of navigating the plethora of toys from the Gifting Tree.

ANALOGY EXPLANATION

In the story, the Gifting Tree's toys represent raw data in the world of machine learning. Just like how these toys don't come with any labels or categories, in unsupervised learning, we work with data that hasn't been labeled, classified, or characterized.

Mia's task of organizing the toys without any prior knowledge is the essence of unsupervised learning. By recognizing patterns, similarities, and differences, Mia (the machine learning algorithm) was able to segment the toys (data) into meaningful groups (clusters). This process mirrors clustering methods in unsupervised learning, where data is grouped based on inherent structures.

Furthermore, the inhabitants' ease of navigation post-organization signifies the real-world advantage of unsupervised learning: extracting structure and patterns from unlabelled data, providing insight, and simplifying navigation and comprehension.

11.4 EXPLANATION AT THREE LEVELS OF DEPTH

The following descriptions explain "Unsupervised Learning" at three levels of complexity.

SIMPLIFIED

Imagine you have a big box of crayons but they're all mixed up. You don't know the names of each color, but you can see some are similar, like different shades of blue or red. **Unsupervised learning** is like sorting those crayons into groups based on their colors, even if you don't know the exact name of each color. So, you're not told which crayon goes where, but you group them by how they look.

GENERAL

In **unsupervised learning**, we have a lot of data, but none of it is labeled. It's like having a playlist of songs without knowing their genres. The computer tries to figure out patterns or similarities among the data on its own. There are two main ways it does this:

- **Clustering:** This is like grouping songs by their vibes or beats. Maybe slow songs in one group and fast-paced ones in another.

- **Association:** It's finding rules that describe parts of your data. Like, if you tend to listen to Song A, you're likely to also enjoy Song B.

So, unsupervised learning is all about letting the computer figure out the structure or patterns in data by itself.

DETAILED

Unsupervised learning refers to the machine learning tasks where an algorithm is provided data without explicit instructions on what to do with it. The system tries to learn the patterns and the structure from the data without any labeled responses to guide the learning process. The main methodologies include:

- **Clustering:** This involves partitioning the dataset into groups, known as clusters, of similar data points. Methods like K-means or hierarchical clustering are used to find inherent groupings.

- **Dimensionality Reduction:** Techniques like Principal Component Analysis (PCA) or t-Distributed Stochastic Neighbor Embedding (t-SNE) are used to reduce the number of random variables under consideration and can be used to visualize complex data.

- **Association Rule Mining:** This aims to find interesting relationships or associations between variables in large datasets. For example, the Apriori algorithm can be used to find items that are frequently purchased together.

The goal in unsupervised learning is to uncover hidden patterns in data, often to derive meaningful insights or to prepare data for further processing in other machine learning tasks.

CHAPTER 12

UNSUPERVISED LEARNING METHODOLOGIES (CLUSTERING, DIMENSIONALITY REDUCTION, AND ANOMALY DETECTION)

In the next trio of stories, we delve into Unsupervised Learning Methodologies, encompassing Clustering, Dimensionality Reduction, and Anomaly Detection. After each tale, we unravel the embedded analogies. Subsequently, we offer clear explanations, crafted at three layers of detail, helping readers gradually enhance their grasp.

12.1 STORY: "THE MYSTERY OF THE LOST LIBRARY"

IN the kingdom of Bibliopolis, there was a legendary library said to contain the wisdom of the ages. However, the library had been lost to time and memory. Its vast chambers, containing millions of books, were hidden underground, waiting to be rediscovered.

One day, three explorers — Clara, Dmitri, and Aria — embarked on an expedition to uncover this lost library.

1. *Clara's Method: The Book Clubs (Clustering)*

When they first entered the library, they were overwhelmed by the vast number of books. Clara decided to organize informal book clubs. She noticed some books were about history, some about science, and others about art. She placed similar books together, creating little groups or 'clusters'. Soon, explorers could easily find a book on a topic they liked because Clara had grouped them by their themes.

2. *Dmitri's Method: The Magical Lens (Dimensionality Reduction)*

While Clara was busy with her book clubs, Dmitri found a magical lens. When he looked through it, he saw not the detailed content of each book, but rather a summary of its essence. Instead of seeing every word on every page, he saw a representation of the main idea. By using the lens, he could quickly understand the core message of any book without reading it in detail. He had reduced the 'dimensionality' of the information, focusing on the essential elements.

3. *Aria's Method: The Mismatched Volumes (Anomaly Detection)*

Aria, with her sharp eyes, began to notice something odd. In some clusters, there were books that didn't quite fit in. For instance, in a group of science books, she found a lone poetry book. These 'anomalies' or 'outliers' caught her attention. She

Figure 12.1: Prompt: A mysterious library in digital art style

began to set these books aside, creating a collection of mismatched volumes. These were the unique treasures of the library, offering unexpected wisdom.

By the end of their expedition, the trio had not only rediscovered the library but had also devised methods to navigate its vast wisdom.

ANALOGY EXPLANATION

- *Clustering*: Just like Clara's book clubs grouped similar books together, clustering in unsupervised learning involves grouping data points that are similar to each other.

- *Dimensionality Reduction*: Dmitri's magical lens that captured the essence of a book is akin to dimensionality reduction techniques like PCA. These methods reduce the number of variables (or 'dimensions') we need to consider, while still retaining the most important information.

- *Anomaly Detection*: Aria's keen observation of books that didn't fit their groups mirrors anomaly detection. This method identifies data points that are significantly different or 'anomalous' compared to the rest of the data.

12.2   STORY: "THE MYSTERY ISLAND EXPEDITION"

Deep in the Pacific Ocean, there's an uncharted mystery island. A group of explorers decided to embark on an expedition to uncover the secrets of this island.

1. *Discovery of Tribes: The Clustering Chronicles* When they reached the island, the explorers noticed groups of indigenous people living in distinct regions. One tribe lived by the coastline, another in the dense forest, and a third on the mountain tops. Though they were all from the same island, each tribe had its own unique culture, attire, and traditions.

2. *Mapping the Essentials: The Cartographer's Compass* The team included cartographer Jane. Jane had a special compass that pointed not to the north but to the most interesting landmarks. The island was vast, and making a detailed map would take years. So, she used her compass to simplify the map, marking only the most essential landmarks. Instead of every tree or rock, her map

Figure 12.2: Prompt: An uncharted island in the ocean in digital art style

showcased the large mountain, the central river, and the dense forests. These landmarks captured the essence of the island.

3. *The Odd Discoveries: Anomalies in Paradise* As they journeyed, the explorers occasionally stumbled upon peculiar things that didn't seem to belong: a snowglobe in the tropical forest, a refrigerator on the mountain peak, and a penguin waddling by the beach. These oddities were anomalies, very different from the usual findings on the island.

ANALOGY EXPLANATION

1. *Clustering*: The tribes on the island represent clusters. Just like the tribes had distinct characteristics and lived separately, clustering in machine learning groups similar data points together based on certain features.

2. *Dimensionality Reduction*: Jane's simplified map represents dimensionality reduction. She reduced the complexity of the island into a few significant landmarks. Similarly, dimensionality reduction techniques, like PCA, simplify complex datasets by focusing on the most informative features.

3. *Anomaly Detection*: The unusual items and creatures on the island are anomalies. Just as these stood out from the typical island environment, anomaly detection in machine learning identifies rare items or events in datasets that look suspiciously different from the rest.

12.3 STORY: "THE ENCHANTED LIBRARY"

IN a land far away, there was an enchanted library that contained books on every topic imaginable. Over the years, the number of books grew so large that even the most dedicated librarians found it challenging to navigate the vast collection. A group of three wizards, Clara, Dante, and Evan, visited this library to help organize it.

Clara's Task - Clustering: Clara noticed that while the books were numerous, many of them discussed similar topics. She cast a spell that would group books with similar content into distinct clusters. After her spell, there were neat piles: one with books about animals, another about planets, another about magical spells, and so on. Now, anyone searching for a specific topic could easily find the cluster it belonged to.

Dante's Task - Dimensionality Reduction: Dante observed that some books were too detailed, making them challenging to read. These books would talk about a dragon's scale color, the exact length of its claws, the temperature of its fire, and more, all in one page. Dante's magic condensed the information. After his spell, a book discussing a dragon would retain essential characteristics like its size and fire's intensity but wouldn't overwhelm the reader with too many details. The essence of the dragon was still captured, but it was now easier to understand.

Evan's Task - Anomaly Detection: While the library was mostly filled with standard books, there were some rare cursed books hidden. These books looked just like any other but caused mischief when read. Evan specialized in identifying things that didn't belong. He cast a spell that illuminated any book that was "different" or unusual in its nature. By the time Evan was done, all the cursed books were identified and safely isolated.

ANALOGY EXPLANATION

1. *Clustering (Clara's magic)*:
   - Represents the process of grouping data based on similarities.
   - Just as Clara grouped books by their content, clustering algorithms group data into subsets so that the data in each subset share common traits.

2. *Dimensionality Reduction (Dante's magic)*:
   - Simplifies complex data while retaining its essence.
   - Dante's condensing of the dragon's many details into a few essential ones is like dimensionality reduction techniques (like PCA) which reduce the number of variables in data while preserving its most significant structures.

3. *Anomaly Detection (Evan's magic)*:
   - Identifies rare items in the data that might be of interest.

Figure 12.3: Prompt: Three wizards in a huge library in digital art style

- Evan's detection of cursed books is akin to anomaly detection algorithms spotting rare or unusual data points in a dataset, which might represent errors, fraud, or other anomalies.

12.4   EXPLANATION AT THREE LEVELS OF DEPTH

The following descriptions explain "unsupervised learning methodologies clustering, dimensionality reduction and anamoly detection" in three levels of detail.

SIMPLIFIED

a) Clustering: Imagine you have a big box of crayons, but they are all mixed up. Clustering is like sorting these crayons into smaller boxes based on their colors, so all the blue crayons are in one box, all the red ones in another, and so on.

b) Dimensionality Reduction: Think of a big, detailed LEGO castle. Now, imagine making a simpler version of that castle using fewer LEGO pieces but still looking like a castle. Dimensionality reduction is like simplifying things but keeping their main idea.

c) Anomaly Detection: Let's say you have a basket of apples, and you want to find if any are rotten. Anomaly detection is like finding that one rotten apple in a bunch of good ones.

GENERAL

a) Clustering: This method is about grouping similar data together. For instance, if you have a music playlist with various genres, clustering can help group songs into categories like rock, jazz, and pop based on their features.

b) Dimensionality Reduction: In data, sometimes we have too much information, some of which might not be very useful.

Dimensionality reduction helps reduce the number of features or information we have to a smaller set that still contains the most important information. It's like summarizing a long book into key points.

c) Anomaly Detection: This is about finding unusual patterns or data points in a dataset. For instance, in credit card fraud detection, anomaly detection can identify unusual transactions that don't fit a user's typical spending pattern.

DETAILED

a) Clustering: Clustering is an unsupervised learning methodology used to partition a dataset into subsets (clusters) based on similarity, ensuring that data in each subset share common traits. Algorithms like K-means, Hierarchical clustering, and DBSCAN define these groups based on mathematical criteria and distance measures.

b) Dimensionality Reduction: High-dimensional datasets can be problematic due to the curse of dimensionality, which can cause overfitting and increased computational cost. Dimensionality reduction techniques, such as Principal Component Analysis (PCA) or t-distributed Stochastic Neighbor Embedding (t-SNE), transform the original features into a lower-dimensional space, preserving as much of the variance as possible.

c) Anomaly Detection: Anomaly detection techniques are designed to identify outliers or anomalies in a dataset. These outliers could be due to noise, error, or genuinely anomalous behavior. Techniques include statistical tests, machine learning models like One-Class SVM, and neural networks like autoencoders. Such methods are crucial in fields like fraud detection, network security, and quality control.

Chapter 13

Unsupervised Learning Clustering Algorithms (K-means, Hierarchical, and DBSCAN)

In the next trio of stories, we delve into Unsupervised Learning Clustering Algorithms, specifically highlighting K-means, Hierarchical, and DBSCAN. After each tale, we unravel the embedded analogies. Subsequently, we offer clear explanations, crafted at various levels of complexity to incrementally enhance the reader's understanding.

13.1 STORY: "THE ISLAND OF UNIQUE VILLAGES"

O N a distant island, there were inhabitants who had never interacted with the outside world. A team of explorers arrived, wanting to understand the unique cultures and ways of life on this island. The team had three members: Kate, Harry, and Daisy.

1. Kate and the Circle Approach (K-means): Kate had a unique way of making friends. She would find a group of inhabitants, give one of them a flag and declare that person as the 'leader'. Over time, people close to the leader would gather around them, forming a village. Kate would then move to another part of the island and repeat this until there were multiple villages, each with its leader. People in the same village were somewhat similar to each other in their customs and ways.

2. Harry and the Tree Family (Hierarchical Clustering): Harry, on the other hand, believed in connections. He saw the entire island as one big family tree. He started by considering each inhabitant as a separate village. He then began merging the most similar villagers, creating households. These households then merged to form extended families, which joined to make clans, and so on. This process resulted in a family tree of villages, where one could trace back to see which villages merged together in the past.

3. Daisy and the Dense Forest Strategy (DBSCAN): Daisy loved dense forests. She noticed that inhabitants living in dense forest regions had a lot in common. So, she marked dense areas of the island as one village, leaving out sparse regions. When she found a dense area, she'd identify it as a village and then look for nearby dense regions to expand that village. Those who lived in sparser regions, away from the main groups, were considered unique or outliers and were not part of any village.

Figure 13.1: Prompt: An island with distant villages

Analogy Explanation

1. *K-means*: This algorithm works by selecting 'centroids' (leaders in the story) and then assigning data points to the nearest centroid, forming clusters (villages). The position of centroids changes iteratively to minimize the distance between data points and their corresponding centroid.

2. *Hierarchical Clustering*: This method builds a hierarchy or a tree of clusters. It can be agglomerative (like in the story, starting with individual points and combining them) or divisive (starting with one large cluster and dividing it).

3. *DBSCAN*: This method identifies dense regions in the data space as clusters. Points in low-density areas (sparse regions) are typically treated as noise or outliers. Clusters are formed based on density criteria.

13.2   Story: "The Gathering at Fruitlandia"

In a land called Fruitlandia, there was an annual gathering of all kinds of fruits. Fruits from various regions would come together to join the festivity. It was known as the "Great Fruit Mix." Three local organizers, Kay, Hanna, and Debbie, had the task of grouping these fruits.

Kay's Approach (K-means): Kay decided to host a competition. She placed a few baskets (K number of baskets) in the grand field of Fruitlandia. When the whistle blew, each fruit would roll into the basket that was closest to them. After everyone settled, Kay would check the average position of the fruits in each basket and move the basket to that spot. She'd whistle again, and the fruits would once again move to the nearest basket. This process would repeat until the fruits no longer moved between baskets. After a few rounds, all the fruits were nicely grouped in their respective baskets.

Hanna's Approach (Hierarchical): Hanna, on the other hand, wanted a family tree of fruits. She started by saying that every fruit was its own group. Then, she began pairing the closest fruits together, forming tiny groups. She continued this, combining the closest groups or fruits together, again and again, until there was a big family tree showcasing which fruits were closer in relation and which were distant cousins.

Debbie's Approach (DBSCAN): Debbie had a unique strategy. She gave each fruit a circle of a certain size. If a fruit had a minimum number of other fruits in its circle, it became a core fruit. Other fruits close to this core fruit would join its group. Some fruits, close to the core but not having enough neighbors of their own, were border fruits – they joined the group but didn't form their own. And then, some fruits were too far from any group; they remained alone, the outliers.

ANALOGY EXPLANATION

1. *K-means*:
   - *Baskets*: Initial cluster centers.
   - *Rolling towards the nearest basket*: Assigning data points to the nearest cluster center.
   - *Moving the basket to the average position*: Updating the cluster center based on the mean of the data points in it.

   2. *Hierarchical*:
   - *Every fruit its own group*: Each data point is treated as a single cluster.
   - *Pairing the closest fruits*: Agglomerative method of combining two nearest clusters.
   - *Big family tree*: The dendrogram representing the hierarchy of clusters.

   3. *DBSCAN*:

Figure 13.2: Prompt: A festival about different kinds of fruits in a town in digital art style

- *Circle around a fruit*: Epsilon ε radius defining the neighborhood around a data point.

- *Core fruit*: A data point with a minimum number of other data points MinPts within its ε radius.

- *Border fruits*: Data points within the ε radius of a core point but not having MinPts within their own ε radius.

- *Outliers*: Data points not part of any core or border group.

13.3 STORY: "THE GREAT BIRDWATCHING ADVENTURE"

THree friends, Kate, Harry, and Dave, decided to go birdwatching. Each had a different method for identifying and grouping the birds they saw.

1. Kate's K-means Method: Kate brought a pair of binoculars and a notebook. She decided to count the most common colors of birds she saw. If she saw many blue, green, and yellow birds, she would draw three circles in her notebook, one for each color. Then, for each bird she spotted, she would place a dot inside the circle of its predominant color. If a purple bird appeared (a mix of blue and red), she'd place it closer to the blue circle. Over time, these dots formed groups or 'clusters', each centered around her initial colors.

2. Harry's Hierarchical Approach: Harry, always the organized one, brought a family tree chart. He believed every bird was related to another. When he saw two birds that looked quite similar, he would connect them with a line, like siblings. As the day went on, he connected similar pairs or groups to other pairs or groups, forming a big tree structure. At the end of the day, by looking at the topmost connections, he could see major families of birds that had many similarities.

Figure 13.3: Prompt: Three friends, one boy and two girls are birdwatching in digital art style

3. Dave's DBSCAN Dynamics: Dave, the tech geek, brought a drone. He programmed it to fly around and take snapshots of areas where birds were densely populated. He believed that birds of a feather flock together. In areas where birds were densely packed, he'd identify that as a single group. But if a bird was too isolated or far from a dense group, he'd label it as an outlier, saying it doesn't belong to any specific group.

ANALOGY EXPLANATION

- *Kate's K-means Method* is akin to the K-means clustering algorithm. It starts with a predefined number of clusters (the colors) and then assigns data points (birds) to the nearest cluster based on certain attributes, iteratively refining the cluster centers.

- *Harry's Hierarchical Approach* mirrors Hierarchical clustering. This algorithm builds a tree of clusters. It can start by treating each point as a separate cluster and then merging them, or start with a single cluster and divide it up.

- *Dave's DBSCAN Dynamics* is analogous to the DBSCAN algorithm. It identifies dense regions in the data space where many data points are close together, treating less dense regions as noise or outliers.

13.4   EXPLANATION AT THREE LEVELS OF DEPTH

The following descriptions explain "Unsupervised Learning Clustering Algorithms (K-means, Hierarchical, DBSCAN" at three levels of depth.

SIMPLIFIED

Imagine you have a big box of colorful marbles. You want to sort these marbles.

- **K-means**: Imagine asking your friend to close their eyes and pick a few marbles at random. Then, all other marbles that are similar in color get placed near the chosen marbles. Repeat this until all marbles have a group.

- **Hierarchical**: Imagine drawing a family tree for these marbles. You start by saying every marble is its own family. Then, marbles that are really close in color get linked together as siblings. As you keep linking, you end up with a big family tree that shows which groups of marbles are similar.

- **DBSCAN**: Imagine you put all your marbles on the floor. If many marbles are close together, they become a group. If a marble is all by itself or far away from a group, it's left out.

General

You're sorting data points based on similarity.

- **K-means**: Pick a certain number of points randomly as starting 'centroids'. Group data points based on which centroid they are closest to. Adjust the centroids based on the average of their group and repeat until the centroids don't move much.

- **Hierarchical**: Start with each data point as its own cluster. Then, repeatedly merge the closest clusters together. In the end, you get a tree-like diagram called a dendrogram that shows the order in which clusters were merged.

- **DBSCAN**: Group data points that are closely packed together, based on some distance measurement and a minimum number of points. Data points in low-density areas are marked as outliers.

Detailed

- **K-means**: This is a centroid-based algorithm. You initialize k centroids and assign each data point to the nearest centroid, which forms k clusters. Then, you recompute the centroid of each cluster. The process is iteratively repeated until the within-cluster variance can't be decreased further. One limitation is that you need to specify k upfront, and it's sensitive to the initialization of the centroids.

- **Hierarchical**: This algorithm builds a multi-level hierarchy of clusters by creating a cluster tree called a dendrogram. The root of the tree consists of a single cluster containing all samples. The leaves are clusters with only one sample. Two main strategies here are agglomerative (bottom-up) and divisive (top-down). The main challenge is its quadratic runtime complexity, which makes it less scalable for large datasets.

- **DBSCAN (Density-Based Spatial Clustering of Applications with Noise)**: This method divides the dataset into dense and sparse regions. For each point, if there are at least 'minPts' within a given radius 'eps', a new cluster is started. The algorithm can discover clusters of various shapes, not limited to spherical (like K-means). One advantage is that you don't need to specify the number of clusters upfront, but choosing appropriate values for 'eps' and 'minPts' can be challenging.

CHAPTER 14

PRINCIPAL COMPONENT ANALYSIS

In the following three stories, we demystify the concept of 'Principal Component Analysis'. After the tales, we unravel their intricate analogies. We then provide lucid explanations providing details at three different levels to steadily enhance the reader's comprehension.

14.1 STORY: "THE ART SHOW AND THE OVERWHELMING GALLERY"

IN a quaint town named DataVille, there was an annual art show where artists from all around the town would come and present their paintings. Emily, an art enthusiast, visited the show every year and loved looking at the hundreds of paintings displayed.

This year, however, there were thousands of paintings, spread over a massive gallery. As Emily entered, she felt overwhelmed. How could she possibly appreciate and interpret the essence of so many artworks in just a day? It felt impossible to discern the main themes and styles with so many paintings in view.

Seeing her dilemma, an elderly artist named Mr. Mathison approached her. He gave her a special pair of glasses and said, "Wear these. They'll help you see things differently."

When Emily wore the glasses, she couldn't believe her eyes. Instead of thousands of individual paintings, she saw a smaller number of representative artworks, each capturing the essence and style of many similar paintings. Some showed the dominant colors that were popular that year, while others captured recurring patterns or common themes.

With the glasses on, Emily could easily understand and appreciate the main trends and styles of the art show without feeling overwhelmed. She thanked Mr. Mathison for the unique experience. He smiled and said, "It's all about finding the right perspective to capture the essence."

ANALOGY EXPLANATION

In this story:

- The massive gallery with thousands of paintings represents a dataset with many variables.

- Emily's initial overwhelm symbolizes the challenges of understanding and interpreting high-dimensional data.

- The special glasses given by Mr. Mathison represent PCA.

- The fewer, representative artworks that Emily sees through the glasses symbolize the principal components. These artworks (or principal components) capture the essence and variability of the larger dataset, allowing for easier interpretation and analysis.

Just as Emily could appreciate the main styles and themes without having to examine every single painting, PCA allows us to understand the main features and variability of a dataset without analyzing every single variable.

Figure 14.1: Prompt: An art show and an overwhelming gallery in digital art style

14.2   STORY: "THE ART GALLERY AND THE CURIOUS TOURIST"

IN the vibrant city of Mathville, there was a famous art gallery known as "The Data Spectrum." This gallery was renowned for its vast collection of paintings. However, the gallery had a unique challenge: it had limited wall space and too many paintings to display.

One day, a curious tourist named Lucy visited the gallery. She was keen to understand and appreciate the essence of the entire collection in the short time she had. Seeing her keen interest, the gallery curator introduced her to a magical pair of glasses named "PCA Vision."

Lucy wore the glasses and suddenly, instead of thousands of paintings, she saw just a few masterpieces on the walls. These weren't the original paintings but a representation of them. Each masterpiece combined the essence of hundreds of other paintings in a way that captured their most distinguishing features.

For instance, where there were ten paintings of landscapes with slight variations in light, using the glasses, Lucy saw just one painting capturing the most significant light patterns. Similarly, numerous portraits with different expressions were distilled into one or two that captured the predominant emotions.

Amazed, Lucy said, "It feels like I've seen the soul of this gallery in such a short time!" The curator smiled, "That's the power of 'PCA Vision.' It helps you focus on the most impactful elements, giving you a deeper understanding without being overwhelmed."

ANALOGY EXPLANATION

In this story, "The Data Spectrum" art gallery represents a dataset with a lot of variables (or features). The challenge of limited wall

Figure 14.2: Prompt: A woman visitor wearing a pair of glasses in an art gallery in digital art style

space mirrors the challenges of understanding and visualizing data with too many variables.

The magical glasses, "PCA Vision," represent the Principal Component Analysis. When Lucy wears the glasses, she sees fewer paintings, similar to how PCA reduces the dimensions of data. The masterpieces Lucy sees capture the essence of many paintings, much like how principal components capture the maximum variance in data by combining original features.

The experience Lucy has is akin to someone using PCA on a dataset: simplifying and concentrating information, making it easier to understand and analyze without losing the essence.

14.3   STORY: "THE SHADOW PUPPET THEATRE"

IN a quaint little town, there was an annual festival where artists from around the world would showcase their talents. Among them was Maria, a renowned shadow puppeteer. Each year, she'd put on a mesmerizing show that had everyone, from children to the elderly, in awe.

One year, Maria decided to narrate the story of a dense forest filled with a myriad of creatures. There were birds, animals, trees, rivers, and countless more entities. The challenge, however, was that her theatre screen wasn't large enough to depict the entire forest and all its complexities.

Maria had an idea. She decided to illuminate the forest from a certain angle with her light source. This way, the shadows of the most significant parts of the forest - the large trees, the prominent animals, and the flowing rivers - were clearly depicted on her screen. While the smaller bushes and minor creatures were still there, they blended into the larger shadows and became a part of the bigger picture.

Figure 14.3: Prompt: A shadow puppet theatre displaying a show of a forest in digital art style.

The audience was captivated. They saw the essence of the forest without getting overwhelmed by every single detail. They understood the major players and their interactions, and the story was clear and engaging.

ANALOGY EXPLANATION

The dense forest is a dataset with many variables (or dimensions). Just as it's hard to showcase every creature and plant in the forest on a small screen, it's challenging to visualize and understand datasets with many dimensions.

Maria's solution, using the light to cast prominent shadows, is akin to *Principal Component Analysis (PCA)*. PCA shines a metaphorical light on the data to find the "best angle" (or components) that captures the most information (or variance). The most significant shadows (principal components) represent combinations of the original variables that capture the essence of the data.

Just as the audience could understand the forest's main story without knowing every minor detail, PCA allows data scientists to work with and visualize the most important aspects of a dataset without getting lost in the complexity of every variable.

14.4 EXPLANATIONS AT THREE LEVELS OF DEPTH

The following descriptions explain "Principal Component Analysis (PCA)" at three levels of complexity.

SIMPLIFIED

Imagine you have a box and you look at it from the top. All the items mix together, and you can't tell which is which. But if you tilt the box a certain way, you can see more items clearly. PCA is like finding the best way to tilt your box so you can see the most items at once without them overlapping too much.

GENERAL

You've got a spreadsheet full of data, and it has many columns. It's overwhelming to look at everything at once. PCA is like finding the most important columns that tell you the most about your data. Instead of 10 or 20 columns, you can just look at 2 or 3, making it simpler to understand and visualize. These new columns are a combination of the old ones and show you the biggest differences in your data.

DETAILED

PCA is a statistical procedure that utilizes orthogonal transformation to convert a set of observations of possibly correlated variables into a set of linearly uncorrelated variables called principal components. The first principal component captures the most variance in the dataset, the second (orthogonal to the first) captures the second most, and so on. Essentially, PCA reduces the dimensionality of the dataset, concentrating its variance into fewer dimensions. It's particularly useful for visualization, noise filtering, feature extraction, and more. It's important to note that while PCA can make the data easier to understand and work with, there's a risk of losing some information when reducing dimensions.

Chapter 15

Semi-supervised Learning

In the next trio of stories, we peel back the layers of the 'semi-supervised learning' concept. After these narratives, we decode the rich analogies woven into each tale. We then follow up with clear and approachable explanations, designed to be enlightening for readers of all ages by providing three levels of detail to enhance their understanding step by step.

15.1 Story: "The Young Botanist"

ONCE upon a time in a small village, there was a young girl named Lina who loved plants. Her dream was to become a great botanist. One day, her teacher gave her a special assignment: she had to categorize all the plants in the school's garden into medicinal and non-medicinal plants.

Her teacher gave her a book that had pictures and descriptions of 10 different plants, 5 of which were medicinal and 5 of which were non-medicinal. The garden, however, had 100 different kinds of plants! Lina was initially overwhelmed, but she decided to approach the task methodically.

First, she studied the 10 plants in the book thoroughly. She noticed certain patterns: medicinal plants often had a particular type of leaf shape and a specific kind of flower.

The next day, she went to the garden and started looking for plants that matched the patterns she had learned from the book. To her delight, she found 30 plants that closely resembled the medicinal plants in her book.

She then showed these plants to her teacher, who confirmed that Lina's observations were correct for 25 of the plants but incorrect for 5. Lina took note of her mistakes, went back to the garden, and adjusted her criteria based on the feedback.

With her refined understanding, she continued her quest and was able to classify a significant number of the remaining plants as either medicinal or non-medicinal. When she had gone through all the plants, her teacher was impressed with her accuracy and determination. Lina was not only able to complete her assignment but also discovered a few plants that were previously unknown to have medicinal properties. Her teacher was so impressed that she decided to add Lina's findings to a new edition of the book.

ANALOGY EXPLANATION

In this story:

- *Lina* is the *machine learning algorithm* in semi-supervised learning.

- The *10 plants in the book with known properties (medicinal or non-medicinal)* represent the *labeled data* in semi-supervised learning. This is the small portion of the data where we know the output or category.

- The *100 different plants in the garden* represent the entire *dataset*, including both labeled and unlabeled data.

Figure 15.1: Prompt: A young botanist girl in a colorful botanic garden in digital art style

- Lina's *initial observation and categorization of plants based on patterns she learned from the book* mimic how a semi-supervised learning algorithm first *trains on a small set of labeled data.*

- When Lina *identified other plants in the garden that resembled the medicinal plants in her book, she was essentially labeling the unlabeled data,* akin to how the algorithm makes *predictions on the unlabeled data based on what it learned from the labeled data.*

- Lina's *teacher confirming or correcting her classifications* is similar to the *pseudo-labels in semi-supervised learning being refined.* In a real-world scenario, some of these pseudo-labels might be checked and corrected by a human expert, or the algorithm might use statistical techniques to estimate the reliability of its pseudo-labels.

- Lina *going back to the garden with refined criteria* after feedback from her teacher is akin to the *iterative nature of semi-supervised learning,* where the model is *re-trained with the augmented dataset (original labeled data + pseudo-labeled data),* and the process may repeat to improve the model's accuracy further.

- In the end, Lina's work helps to *expand and improve the knowledge represented in the book,* just as a semi-supervised learning algorithm can help to *improve a predictive model by effectively leveraging unlabeled data.*

This story illustrates how, with a small amount of initial guidance (the labeled data), one can learn patterns that help to make educated guesses about a much larger set of unknown information (the unlabeled data), and how this process can be refined iteratively to improve accuracy.

15.2 STORY: "THE LOST PUPPIES"

ONce upon a time in a quiet town, there was a kind-hearted animal shelter volunteer named Maya. One day, a big storm passed through the town, and several puppies got separated from their families and were lost.

After the storm, Maya found three puppies on her doorstep, each wearing a collar with a name tag and a note that indicated whether they were trained or not. Maya took care of them and noticed how the trained puppies would sit on command, while the untrained ones wouldn't.

The next morning, she heard from the town's folks that more puppies were spotted in various parts of the town, but nobody knew which ones were trained. Seeing the urgency, Maya set off with the three puppies she had.

As they walked through the town, the trained puppies from her home started to play and engage more with some lost puppies they encountered, while keeping distance from others. Observing this, Maya hypothesized that the trained puppies she had were naturally more comfortable around other trained puppies.

Using this insight, she decided to temporarily label the puppies that her trained dogs engaged with as "trained" and the ones they avoided as "untrained."

To test her hypothesis, she picked a few of these newly labeled puppies and gave the "sit" command. As she suspected, the puppies labeled "trained" responded well to the command, confirming her hypothesis was mostly correct.

Encouraged by this, she continued her journey through the town, using her initial three puppies to help label the rest of the lost puppies. By the end of the day, not only did she help rescue all the lost puppies, but she also had a good idea of which puppies were trained and which were not, making it easier for the shelter to care for them appropriately until they could be reunited with their families.

ANALOGY EXPLANATION

In this story:

- *Maya* represents the *machine learning algorithm* in semi-supervised learning.

Figure 15.2: Prompt: A young woman plays with many cute puppies in digital art style.

- The *three puppies on Maya's doorstep with name tags and notes* represent the *labeled data* in semi-supervised learning. This is the small portion of the data where we know the output or category.
- The *lost puppies in various parts of the town* represent the *unlabeled data* in semi-supervised learning. This is the majority of the data where the category or label is unknown.
- Maya's *observation of how her trained puppies interact with the lost puppies* mimics how a semi-supervised learning algorithm uses patterns it learns from the labeled data to make educated guesses, or *pseudo-labels*, for the unlabeled data.
- *Testing her hypothesis with a "sit" command* for a few puppies is akin to the process of *validating the pseudo-labels* generated by the algorithm. In a real-world scenario, some of these pseudo-labels might be checked and confirmed or corrected by human experts or additional data sources.
- Maya *iteratively using her initial three puppies to help label the rest of the lost puppies as she travels through the town* parallels the *iterative nature of semi-supervised learning*. After an initial model is trained on labeled data, it is used to generate pseudo-labels for the unlabeled data, and then the model may be re-trained on the combined data (original labeled data + pseudo-labeled data), improving its performance with each cycle.

This story illustrates how, with a small amount of initial guidance (the labeled data), one can learn patterns or characteristics that help to make educated guesses about a much larger set of unknown information (the unlabeled data), and how this process can be refined iteratively to improve accuracy.

15.3   STORY: "THE ARTIST'S APPRENTICE"

O NCE upon a time in a picturesque village lived a famous artist named Maestro. He was renowned for his remarkable ability to mix colors in a way that made his paintings incredibly lifelike. People traveled from villages near and far to learn from him, and he took in an eager apprentice named Alina.

One day, Maestro received a commission to paint a large mural for the royal family, and he realized this was the perfect opportunity for Alina to learn. He decided to turn this project into a lesson.

Maestro gave Alina a palette with only four colors labeled: blue, red, yellow, and white, and a mission to reproduce the colors in a beautiful flower garden. However, he provided her with a chart of ten mixed colors (e.g., light green, lavender, pink, etc.) and told her explicitly how these ten could be mixed from the base colors.

At first, Alina used the chart diligently. She measured and mixed to recreate the exact colors Maestro had defined. But as she continued her work, she began to notice patterns. For instance, she realized that adding a little white made colors lighter and mixing red and blue in equal parts resulted in a vibrant purple.

Venturing beyond her chart, she started to mix colors for other elements of the garden – the trees, sky, and animals – based on her observations from the initial set of instructions.

Each day, Maestro reviewed her work, offering gentle corrections when the colors were off and praising the hues she'd gotten right. With this guidance, Alina rapidly improved. She learned not only to reproduce the colors on her chart but also to create a vast array of new colors by extrapolating from Maestro's original lessons.

By the time the mural was finished, Alina had mastered the art of color mixing and had played a significant role in the creation

Figure 15.3: Prompt: A young woman painting colorful flowers on a large mural in digital art style.

of a masterpiece. She'd learned not just from direct instruction but from her own experimentation and Maestro's subsequent validation.

ANALOGY EXPLANATION

In this story:

- *Maestro, the famous artist,* symbolizes the *initial model training* phase in semi-supervised learning. He provides a set of labeled examples (the color chart) that are definite and known.

- *Alina, the apprentice*, represents the *machine learning algorithm*.

- The *palette with only four labeled colors* represents the *small set of labeled data* in semi-supervised learning. These are the examples for which we know the correct answer.

- The *chart of ten mixed colors* that Maestro gave to Alina is analogous to the *labeled examples* in a semi-supervised learning dataset. This is a small portion of the data where we know the output or category.

- When *Alina starts to mix colors for other elements of the garden based on her observations*, this is akin to the algorithm *making predictions on unlabeled data* based on the patterns it learned from the labeled data.

- *Maestro's daily review and feedback* are similar to the *refinement process in semi-supervised learning*. The model makes predictions (or pseudo-labels the unlabeled data), and these predictions are then validated and corrected as necessary, forming a feedback loop that helps to improve the model's performance iteratively.

This story illustrates how, with a small set of initial guidance (labeled data), one can learn patterns that enable educated guesses about a much larger set of unknown information (unlabeled data). And through a process of making these guesses and receiving feedback (validation and correction), the learner (or algorithm) can continuously improve and refine its understanding and performance.

15.4   Explanations at Three Levels of Depth

The following descriptions explain "semi-supervised learning" at three levels of depth.

SIMPLIFIED

Imagine you have a big basket of fruits, but only some of them have labels telling whether they are apples or oranges. You already know what apples and oranges generally look like from the few labeled ones. Semi-supervised learning is like looking at the labeled fruits (the ones we know are apples or oranges) and using what we learned from them to help us guess what the unlabeled fruits in the basket are. It's like being a fruit detective, using clues from the fruits we know to solve the mystery of the unlabeled fruits!

GENERAL

In semi-supervised learning, we use a small amount of labeled data (where we know the answer) and a large amount of unlabeled data (where we don't know the answer) to train a machine learning model. Think of it like a science experiment where you have only a few samples where you know the result and many more samples without results. We start with the samples for which we know the results (labeled data), and we use that knowledge to make educated guesses about the unknown samples (unlabeled data). Then, we use these educated guesses to improve our original experiment, making it smarter and more accurate. This way, even with a small amount of known data, we can still learn a lot and make accurate predictions.

DETAILED

Semi-supervised learning (SSL) is a machine learning paradigm that leverages a small set of labeled data and a large set of unlabeled data for model training. The core hypothesis in SSL is that the unlabeled data, although lacking explicit annotations, still contains useful information that can help in learning the underlying data distribution more effectively.

Here's how it typically works:

- First, a model is trained using the available labeled data. This is often a small dataset, but it is crucial since it provides the initial guidance to the model about the task at hand (e.g., classification, regression).

- The trained model is then used to predict the labels of the unlabeled data. Depending on the approach, only the most confident predictions may be used.

- These pseudo-labeled data points are then combined with the original labeled dataset, forming an augmented dataset.

- The model is re-trained on this augmented dataset, refining its parameters based on the additional data.

- This process might be iterative, with the model's predictions on the unlabeled data becoming increasingly reliable with each pass.

Several approaches are used in SSL, such as self-training, multi-view learning, and label propagation. SSL is particularly effective when acquiring a fully labeled dataset is expensive or impractical, but unlabeled data is abundant and cheap. By integrating unlabeled data into the training process, SSL algorithms aim to improve the model's generalization performance, making more accurate predictions on new, unseen data.

Theoretical frameworks for SSL are often grounded in the assumption that similar data points are likely to share the same label (smoothness assumption) and that the data lies on a lower-dimensional manifold within the high-dimensional space (manifold assumption). These assumptions help to formalize why and when SSL can be expected to improve upon supervised learning with only labeled data.

CHAPTER 16

SELF-SUPERVISED LEARNING

In the upcoming set of three stories, we unravel the mysteries of the 'self-supervised learning' concept. Following each narrative, we dissect the thoughtfully crafted analogies embedded within. We conclude with concise and accessible explanations, aimed to shed light on the topic at three levels of detail for readers to gradually enhance their comprehension.

16.1 STORY: "SARAH AND THE MYSTERY ISLAND MAP"

Once upon a time, in a small coastal village, lived a young girl named Sarah. One day, she found a worn-out map in her grandmother's attic. The map was of a mysterious island, but unlike any map Sarah had seen before, this one had no names or labels on it – just lines that represented roads, and symbols for mountains, rivers, and forests. However, intriguingly, there was a dotted line leading from the island's shore to a marked 'X' that seemed to indicate a hidden treasure.

Sarah was eager and curious. She decided she would embark on an adventure to find this treasure. But she had a problem: she didn't know what any of the symbols on the map meant, nor where exactly this island was. Instead of giving up, Sarah decided to be resourceful. She began by comparing the mystery map with other labeled maps from her grandmother's collection, looking for matching patterns and features.

First, she noticed a similarity between the shape of the coastline on her map and one in another map of an island her grandmother had visited. Encouraged, Sarah then started to notice other patterns: a certain symbol that appeared near water in the labeled maps also appeared near the coasts and rivers in her mystery map, so she guessed it might mean "bridge". A cluster of small rectangles inland she hypothesized to be buildings or a village, as she saw similar clusters in populated areas on the other maps.

As Sarah made these connections, she began writing her own labels on the mystery map based on her observations. She used her newfound understanding to plan her route along the dotted line towards the 'X', using the other maps as her guide to navigate the terrain and landmarks she had labeled.

After a week of preparation, Sarah set sail towards the island. To her delight, as she arrived and ventured inland, she found that most of her labels were accurate. The bridges were where she expected, and the path she had planned led her through a village, just as she had guessed. Finally, following her self-annotated map, she reached the marked 'X', where she unearthed a chest containing her grandmother's old journals and artifacts from her travels.

The adventure turned out to be a heartwarming journey into her grandmother's past, and Sarah had solved the mystery using the unlabeled map and her own resourcefulness.

Figure 16.1: Prompt: A young woman looking into an old mysterious treasure map in digital art style

ANALOGY EXPLANATION

In this story:

- *Sarah* symbolizes a *machine learning model.*

- The *mystery map* that Sarah found represents the *unlabeled data* in self-supervised learning.

- The process of *comparing the mystery map with labeled maps from her grandmother's collection* represents the *pretext task* in self-supervised learning, where the model is learning useful features or representations from the data itself without explicit labels.

- *Writing her own labels on the mystery map* based on the patterns and symbols she recognized is analogous to the *latent representations* that a self-supervised learning model infers from the data. These representations are valuable and can be used for various tasks, similar to how Sarah's labels helped her navigate to the treasure.

- *Sarah's journey to the island and her successful navigation using her annotated map* resembles the *downstream tasks* in machine learning, where the representations learned through self-supervised learning are applied to new, but related tasks (like classification or anomaly detection), often with some additional supervision or fine-tuning.

- The *treasure, in the end,* symbolizes the *valuable insights or predictions* that can be obtained after the model has learned meaningful representations of the data through self-supervised learning.

This story illustrates how, with self-supervised learning, a machine can teach itself to understand and interpret data by creating its own labels or representations, which can then be applied effectively to related tasks where specific outcomes or predictions are desired.

16.2 STORY: "TIM AND THE SECRET LANGUAGE"

IN a quiet, rural town lived a young boy named Tim. One summer, Tim discovered a series of intriguing and beautifully written letters in the attic of his home. The letters were written in a language he couldn't understand, filled with symbols and characters completely foreign to him. Tim learned from his parents that these letters were written by his great-grandfather, who had created a secret language for fun.

Fascinated and inspired, Tim decided he would learn this secret language, but there was no dictionary or guidebook. However, in the collection of letters, Tim noticed that some of the letters had corresponding translations written in English, likely drafted by his great-grandfather for practice. These translations only covered a small fraction of the total letters, though.

With his limited set of translated letters, Tim started to notice patterns. For instance, certain symbols appeared frequently at the end of sentences – he guessed these might be punctuation marks. Other symbols appeared commonly next to names, which he deduced might be the word "and" or conjunctions in this language.

To decipher the language, Tim devised a game. He took a translated letter and covered the English text, trying to translate it himself using the patterns he'd observed. He would then uncover the English version to check how many words he got right, adjust his understanding based on what he learned, and repeat the process with the next letter.

Over time, and through this self-created feedback loop, Tim began to understand more and more of the secret language. Eventually, he could read and understand most of the untranslated

Figure 16.2: Prompt: A young boy reading letters with great interest in an attic in digital art style.

letters, unraveling heartfelt stories and wise lessons his great-grandfather had written.

At the end of the summer, Tim compiled a dictionary for this secret language from the patterns and translations he had figured out himself, turning the unknown into the known, the foreign into the familiar.

ANALOGY EXPLANATION

In this story:

- *Tim* represents a *machine learning model*.

- The *secret language* in the letters symbolizes the *complex, high-dimensional data* that the model is trying to learn from.

- The *small set of translated letters* corresponds to a *pretext task* that the model can learn from. These are tasks designed to be self-supervised, where the input data itself provides the supervision, without requiring separate external labels.

- *Tim's process of guessing the translation based on patterns*, and then checking his guess against the actual translation, is analogous to a self-supervised learning algorithm *making predictions and then refining its model based on how those predictions compare to the actual data.*

- *Tim's compiled dictionary* at the end represents the *learned feature representations* that the machine learning model has acquired through self-supervised learning. Just as Tim could understand new letters using the knowledge he compiled, a self-supervised learning model can apply its learned representations to new, unseen data.

- *Unraveling heartfelt stories and wise lessons* symbolizes the *valuable insights or predictions* that can be obtained after the model has learned meaningful representations of the data through self-supervised learning.

This story illustrates how, in self-supervised learning, a model learns to understand data by creating its own feedback loop from a portion of the data itself, without needing extensive labeled examples. It emphasizes the creative and iterative nature of this learning process, as the model (or Tim, in our story) refines its understanding continuously based on the patterns it discovers.

16.3   Story: "Luna and the Colorful Garden"

IN a small village surrounded by vast fields and bright, blooming flowers lived a young girl named Luna. Luna loved painting, and her biggest dream was to paint the most beautiful garden anyone had ever seen. There was just one problem: Luna was colorblind.

One day, Luna discovered a set of paint cans in her grandmother's shed. Each can was labeled, but only in a language Luna didn't understand. Luna knew, however, that these were the special paints her grandmother used to create vibrant gardens on canvas, and she was determined to use them herself.

So Luna came up with a plan. She decided to use the texture of each paint to learn how to identify them. She noticed that each paint had a distinct feel to it: some were smooth, others grainy, some thick and others thin. Luna spent hours every day touching the paints and guessing their colors based on their textures.

After a few weeks, Luna's grandmother, who was fluent in the language of the labels, visited her. Luna asked her grandmother to set up a few "tests" for her: her grandmother would pick a paint can, write down the color in Luna's language, and then Luna would try to guess the color based on the texture. Luna's grandmother was impressed—Luna guessed correctly most of the time!

Seeing Luna's determination and the unique skill she had developed, her grandmother translated all the labels for her. With this newfound knowledge, Luna started painting. She painted gardens with vibrant, accurate colors, each stroke filled with confidence. Her paintings were so breathtaking that people from all around came to see them. Luna, despite being colorblind, had learned to create a colorful world through her art.

Figure 16.3: Prompt: A young girl painting gardens on a canvas with vibrant colors in digital art style.

ANALOGY EXPLANATION

In this story:
- *Luna* represents a *machine learning model*.
- *Being colorblind* symbolizes the model's initial *lack of labels or annotations* for the data it is presented with.
- The *paint cans with labels in an unknown language* represent *raw, unlabeled data*.
- *Luna's method of understanding the paint colors based on their textures* represents the *pretext task* in self-supervised learning. She creates a task (guessing the color based on texture) that is related to what she ultimately wants to do (paint beautiful gardens), but doesn't require knowing the actual colors (labels) upfront. This is similar to how self-supervised learning models learn useful representations from data without requiring explicit labels.
- *Luna's grandmother's tests* where she validates Luna's guesses symbolize the *evaluation or fine-tuning step* in machine learning where the learned features are tested and refined using a smaller labeled dataset.
- *Luna's ability to paint vibrant gardens after understanding the paints* represents the *use of learned representations for downstream tasks*. Just as Luna could create beautiful paintings based on her understanding of paint textures, a self-supervised learning model can apply its learned representations to perform well on tasks that require labels (like classification, detection, etc.), once it has access to that information.

This story illustrates how self-supervised learning allows a machine to develop a useful understanding of data without explicit labels, by framing a task (like Luna's texture-color association) where the data itself provides supervisory signals. This learned understanding can later be refined and employed effectively for tasks where specific outcomes or labels are of interest.

16.4 EXPLANATIONS AT THREE LEVELS OF DEPTH

The following descriptions explain "Self-supervised Learning" in different levels of complexity.

SIMPLIFIED

Imagine you have a big picture book, and each page of the book has a colorful picture and a sentence that describes the picture. Now, let's say all the sentences are cut out from the book and mixed up. Your task is to match each sentence back with the correct picture it describes. While doing this, you are learning what different words mean based on the pictures they match with, without anyone telling you directly. In a similar way, self-supervised learning is when a computer teaches itself to understand something by finding patterns, without being directly told what those patterns mean.

GENERAL

Self-supervised learning is a way to train a computer program to get better at a task without directly supervising it. Imagine you're given a big jigsaw puzzle, but without the picture on the box. You start putting pieces together based on the shapes and colors of the pieces, figuring out how they connect. Slowly, as you put more pieces together, you start to see the bigger picture. In self-supervised learning, a computer program is given a task (like solving a jigsaw puzzle) derived from the data itself (like the shapes and colors of the puzzle pieces), without any additional labels or information. The computer uses this task to learn about the structure and patterns in the data, and this knowledge can later be used for other tasks where labels or additional information are available.

Detailed

Self-supervised learning is a paradigm within machine learning where models are trained to predict or reconstruct part of the input data from other parts of the input data. In this setting, the data itself provides supervision, without the need for explicit external labels. For example, in natural language processing, a common self-supervised task is to predict a word in a sentence given the surrounding words (like the task in Word2Vec or BERT models), or to predict the next sentence given a sequence of sentences. These models learn rich representations of the data through these pretext tasks, which can then be fine-tuned for downstream tasks (like classification or translation) that have labeled data. The major advantage of self-supervised learning is that it can leverage large amounts of unlabeled data to pre-train models, which can be especially valuable when labeled data is scarce or expensive to obtain.

CHAPTER 17

FEATURE ENGINEERING

In the forthcoming trio of tales, we delve into the nuances of the 'feature engineering' idea. After each story, we break down the artfully interwoven analogies present in them. We wrap up with succinct and reader-friendly interpretations, intended to illuminate the subject for everyone by providing the same concept at three levels of detail to progressively deepen the understanding.

17.1 STORY: "CHEF ANTONIO AND THE PERFECT PASTA SAUCE"

IN a small coastal town in Italy, lived Chef Antonio, known far and wide for his remarkable pasta sauces. One day, a culinary school decided to host a competition for the best pasta sauce, and Antonio decided to participate.

In his kitchen, Antonio had a huge shelf full of ingredients: tomatoes, garlic, basil, oregano, peppers, onions, and much more. However, he knew that using all of them would overwhelm the taste of the sauce. He needed to pick the most essential ingredients that would harmonize perfectly.

Antonio remembered his grandmother's advice: "To make the sauce magical, balance the sweet, the sour, and the savory." He decided to use ripe tomatoes for sweetness, a dash of balsamic vinegar for sourness, and fresh garlic and basil for savoriness.

He also remembered that finely chopped onions caramelized beautifully, enhancing the sweetness naturally, and that roasting the garlic before adding it mellowed its flavor and enriched the sauce.

On the competition day, the judges were enchanted by Antonio's sauce. It was rich and balanced, neither too sweet nor too sour. Antonio won the competition, not because he used rare ingredients, but because he knew which ingredients to pick and how to prepare them to complement each other perfectly.

ANALOGY EXPLANATION

In this story:

- *Chef Antonio* represents the *data scientist or machine learning engineer*.

- The *shelf full of ingredients* symbolizes the *raw data* available for building a machine learning model. Just like how the shelf has many ingredients, raw data can have a plethora of variables or features.

- Antonio's decision to *pick the most essential ingredients* based on his grandmother's advice parallels the process of *selecting the most informative and relevant features* in a dataset. This is akin to how a data scientist must select the features that are most predictive of the target variable.

- The way Antonio *prepares the onions and garlic* represents *feature transformation* in machine learning, where raw data is processed and transformed to make it more suitable for a model. For example, a data scientist might normalize or scale a numerical feature or encode a categorical feature.

Figure 17.1: Prompt: An Italian chef cooking pasta sauce in digital art style

- *Antonio's grandmother's advice* to balance the sweet, sour, and savory is akin to *domain knowledge* in data science. It's the wisdom or expertise that helps a data scientist know what features are likely to be important and how they might interact with each other.

- The *resulting perfect sauce* that wins the competition symbolizes a *high-performing machine learning model* that makes accurate predictions because of effective feature engineering.

This story illustrates how feature engineering in machine learning, much like crafting a perfect pasta sauce, is about selecting, transforming, and combining raw ingredients (or features) in a way that they complement each other and contribute meaningfully to the final outcome (or prediction). It emphasizes the role of expertise (or domain knowledge) and creativity in this process.

17.2   STORY: "FARMER JANE AND THE PRIZE-WINNING PUMPKINS"

IN a small rural town, there was an annual pumpkin competition. Everyone in town would present their best pumpkins, and the biggest, most vibrant pumpkin would win. Farmer Jane had been participating in the competition for years but never won. She wondered, "What can I do differently to grow a prize-winning pumpkin?"

Jane realized she needed more than just soil, water, and sun. She decided to start a pumpkin-growing journal. In it, she noted down every detail: the amount of sunlight her patch got, the pH level of her soil, the amount of water she used, the type of fertilizer, and when she planted her seeds. She even recorded the music she played to her pumpkins, as she heard it could help plants grow.

After a year, looking at her journal, Jane noticed a pattern. Her pumpkins grew best when the soil was slightly acidic, they received about 6 hours of sun daily, and were watered moderately, not too much or too little.

Excited, Jane decided to get creative. She calculated the average temperature during the growing season, kept a measure of how many bees visited (for pollination), and even noted the moon's phases, as she read it might affect plant growth.

The next year, armed with her carefully engineered "features" from her journal, Jane grew a spectacular pumpkin. It was enormous, vibrant, and healthy. At the competition, her pumpkin was the star, and for the first time, Farmer Jane won the prize.

ANALOGY EXPLANATION

In this story:

- *Farmer Jane* represents a *data scientist or machine learning engineer*.

- The *pumpkin competition* symbolizes the *challenge of building a high-performing machine learning model*.

- Jane's *initial simple approach* (just soil, water, and sun) is akin to a *baseline machine learning model* with minimal features.

- The *pumpkin-growing journal* where Jane records various details represents the *raw data* that a data scientist has at the beginning. This data can be vast and varied.

- Jane's realization that she needs to look beyond the obvious and her decision to *meticulously note down various factors and conditions* represents the process of *creating new features* from existing data, a core aspect of feature engineering.

- Jane's observations about *soil acidity, amount of sunlight, and water* symbolize *feature selection*, where she identifies which features (in this case, conditions for growing pumpkins) are most impactful.

Figure 17.2: Prompt: A pumpkin competition in a rural town in digital art style.

- Jane's creative additions, like *calculating the average temperature, measuring bee visits, and noting moon phases,* represent *advanced feature engineering.* This is akin to creating interaction terms, polynomial features, or other complex transformations of the raw data in machine learning.

- The *prize-winning pumpkin* that Jane grows symbolizes a *high-performing machine learning model*—one that is able to make accurate predictions or classifications due to the carefully engineered features.

This story illustrates how feature engineering in machine learning is akin to a thoughtful, creative, and systematic approach to growing a perfect pumpkin. Just as Jane experiments with various conditions, observes the results, and iteratively refines her approach, a data scientist iteratively experiments with different features, observes the model performance, and refines the features to improve the model. It's about understanding the raw data deeply, selecting the most important variables, and creatively transforming or combining them to help the model learn the underlying patterns effectively.

17.3 STORY: "THE COMPASS CRAFTSMAN"

IN a peaceful harbor town lived an old compass craftsman named Oliver. Oliver was famous throughout the land for his reliable compasses that helped sailors navigate treacherous waters and discover new lands. Each of his compasses was a little different, but they were all masterpieces.

One day, a curious young boy named Ben visited Oliver's workshop and asked, "How do you make such perfect compasses that lead all sailors back home?"

Oliver smiled and decided to reveal his secret to the eager Ben. He took Ben to a room filled with various tools and materials: magnets of different strengths, needles of different lengths, bowls of various sizes and shapes, and an array of dials and scales.

"The secret," Oliver said, "is not in having the most materials, but in selecting the perfect components and preparing them just right."

He demonstrated his process:

1. *Choosing the Right Needle:* Oliver explained that the needle is the core. He would pick a needle that was not too heavy, so it moved easily, but not too light, so it remained steady.

2. *Magnetizing the Needle:* Oliver would then carefully stroke the needle with a magnet, not too many times, but enough to ensure it aligns with the Earth's magnetic field.

3. *Balancing the Dial:* To make sure the needle wouldn't stick, Oliver would meticulously shape and smooth the bowl and ensure the dial was perfectly level.

4. *Calibrating:* Finally, he would test the compass outdoors, comparing its readings with the known directions and adjusting it until it pointed just right.

By the time Oliver finished his explanation, Ben could see why each compass was so special. It wasn't just about the parts; it was about choosing, preparing, and fine-tuning each component to work in harmony.

ANALOGY EXPLANATION

In this story:

- *Compass Craftsman Oliver* represents a *data scientist or machine learning engineer.*

- The *compasses* that Oliver creates are analogous to the *machine learning models* that data scientists build.

Figure 17.3: Prompt: An old man showing a compass in his hand to a young man in digital art style.

- The *room filled with various tools and materials* represents the *raw data* available to a data scientist. Like Oliver's materials, raw data can be diverse and abundant.

- *Choosing the Right Needle* is akin to *selecting important features* in a dataset. Just as Oliver picks a needle that is just right, data scientists must choose features that are informative and relevant, avoiding those that are too noisy or redundant.

- *Magnetizing the Needle* symbolizes the process of *transforming features* to make them more informative or to scale them appropriately. Oliver's careful magnetizing of the needle is parallel to a data scientist transforming and normalizing features to align them better with the target variable.

- *Balancing the Dial* reflects the need for *data preprocessing and cleaning* in machine learning. Just as Oliver ensures the dial and bowl are smooth and level, a data scientist needs to handle missing data, remove outliers, and clean up inconsistencies in the data.

- *Calibrating* the compass is akin to *fine-tuning a machine learning model*. After a model is trained, it often needs to be tested and adjusted—similar to how Oliver tests each compass outdoors and adjusts it to align with the known directions.

This story illustrates that feature engineering in machine learning is a thoughtful, precise process, much like crafting a perfect compass. It is not solely about the amount of data (or materials) one has, but about selecting, transforming, and refining that data into a form that allows the model (or compass) to operate accurately and efficiently. It's a process that combines artistry, science, and a deep understanding of the components at hand.

17.4 EXPLANATIONS AT THREE LEVELS OF DEPTH

The following descriptions explain "Feature Engineering" in three levels of detail.

SIMPLIFIED

Imagine you have a big box of LEGO pieces of all different shapes, sizes, and colors. You want to build a cool robot. Now, you could just grab any pieces and start sticking them together, but your robot might end up looking funny or not standing up straight. Instead, if you carefully pick the best pieces, maybe the flat ones for the feet, the long ones for the arms, and the shiny ones for the eyes, your robot will look way cooler and work better.

Feature engineering is like picking the best LEGO pieces to build your robot. In machine learning, instead of LEGOs, we have pieces of information (like how tall someone is, what their favorite color is, or how many pets they have). By picking and changing the right pieces of information, we can make our machine (or computer program) work better!

GENERAL

Think about when you're baking a cake. The ingredients you use and how you prepare them can make a big difference in how the cake turns out. If you finely chop the nuts, melt the chocolate just right, or decide to add some extra vanilla, your cake might taste better.

In machine learning, "feature engineering" is similar to preparing your ingredients for a cake. It's about taking the raw information (or "data") you have and turning it into something that's easier and better for the computer to understand. This might mean combining two pieces of information, like taking someone's height and weight to calculate their BMI, or changing a piece of information to make it more useful, like turning a person's age into a category (e.g., 'child', 'teenager', 'adult').

By doing this, we help the computer make better predictions or decisions, just like how preparing ingredients properly helps you bake a better cake.

DETAILED

In the realm of machine learning, feature engineering is the process of selecting, transforming, or creating the most relevant variables, or "features," from raw data to improve the performance of predictive models. Given the high dimensionality of many datasets, raw data often contains redundant, irrelevant, or noisy variables that can hamper the performance of a model. Effective feature engineering can enhance the accuracy, efficiency, and interpretability of a model.

This process often requires domain knowledge to identify which features could be most relevant for a particular task. Techniques might include normalization, where features are scaled to a standard range, or one-hot encoding for categorical variables. More complex tasks might involve polynomial features, where interactions between features are taken into account, or dimensionality reduction techniques like Principal Component Analysis.

The aim of feature engineering is not only to improve model performance but also to reduce overfitting, decrease training time, and enhance the generalizability of the model across various datasets. It's an art as much as it is a science, requiring both creativity and analytical thinking to determine the most informative and relevant features for a given machine learning task.

Chapter 18

Bias and Variance Trade-Off

In our upcoming three tales, we traverse the concepts of the bias and variance trade-off. At the end of each narrative, we decode its intricately woven analogies. We then furnish clear explanations, designed to engage readers by exploring the concept at three levels of complexity to progressively increase the understanding.

18.1 Story: "The Archer's Dilemma"

In a quaint village named Aimville, there was an annual archery competition. Two young archers, Ben and Vicky, were well-known for their skills but had contrasting styles.

Ben's Arrows: Ben, every year, shot his arrows all around the target. Some landed on the left, some on the right, some up, some down. They were all over the place but averaged around the center of the target. The villagers often remarked that Ben's aim was "biased" because he never really hit the bullseye directly, but the spread of his shots was minimal.

Vicky's Arrows: Vicky, on the other hand, was a perfectionist. She practiced one specific shot every day. During one competition, she noticed a gusty wind and didn't account for it. As a result, all her arrows consistently landed on the top-left corner of the target. While all her shots were grouped tightly together, showing low spread, they were far from the bullseye. The villagers would say that Vicky's shots had high "variance" since they'd vary drastically with slight changes in conditions.

Over time, both Ben and Vicky realized their shortcomings. Ben worked on reducing his bias, ensuring his average shot was closer to the bullseye, while Vicky trained in diverse conditions to reduce her variance.

However, as they improved, they realized an essential truth: Perfecting one's aim is a delicate balance between bias and variance. Focusing too much on getting the average shot to the bullseye might increase the spread in unpredictable conditions, and over-concentrating on a single style of shooting might make one vulnerable to slight changes.

ANALOGY EXPLANATION

- *Bias (Ben's Arrows)*: Bias refers to the error due to overly simplistic assumptions in the learning algorithm. Just as Ben's arrows were spread around the target, a high bias model oversimplifies the problem, leading to consistent and predictable errors but not necessarily accurate predictions.

- *Variance (Vicky's Arrows)*: Variance refers to the error due to too much complexity in the learning algorithm. Like Vicky's arrows that were consistent but off the mark under new conditions, a high variance model captures random noise in the training data and performs poorly on new, unseen data.

The *trade-off*: In machine learning, there's a trade-off between bias and variance. Aiming for extremely low bias can lead to complex models that have high variance. On the other hand,

Figure 18.1: Prompt: Two young archers in an archer competition in digital art style.

trying to minimize variance might result in a model too simple, leading to high bias. The goal is to find a balance where both bias and variance are reasonably low, resulting in models with good generalization on new, unseen data.

18.2   STORY: "THE ARCHER AND THE TWO COMPETITIONS"

IN a quiet town nestled between mountains, archery was the most popular sport. Every year, two major competitions were held: the Town's Target Tournament and the Forest's Floating Feathers Challenge.

At the *Town's Target Tournament*, archers shot at stationary targets. One young archer, named Ben, always shot arrows that landed very close to each other but often missed the bullseye. People would say, "Ben is very consistent but always slightly off the mark!"

On the other hand, an older archer named Vincent always shot arrows scattered all over the target. Sometimes he'd hit the bullseye, other times he'd miss the target entirely. The townsfolk would remark, "Vincent is unpredictable!"

Then came the *Forest's Floating Feathers Challenge*, where archers aimed at feathers floating down from trees. The constantly moving target required adaptability. Here, Ben struggled a lot. His consistent shots, which were always slightly off from the stationary bullseye, missed the floating feathers entirely. Vincent, with his scattered approach, occasionally hit the feathers since he didn't have a fixed error pattern.

The archery coach, Master Archer Alina, watched them both and commented, "To be the best archer, one must find a balance. Being too consistent can make you rigid, and being too scattered

Figure 18.2: Prompt: A town nestled between mountains in digital art style.

can make you unreliable. The key is to adjust your aim, learning from where the arrow lands each time."

ANALOGY EXPLANATION

- *Ben's Arrows (Bias)*: Ben's arrows consistently missing the bullseye represents high bias in machine learning. A model with high bias oversimplifies the data and consistently gets things wrong, like Ben consistently missing the center of the target. It doesn't capture the complexities of the data.

- *Vincent's Arrows (Variance)*: Vincent's scattered shots signify high variance. A model with high variance is sensitive to small fluctuations in the training data, like Vincent's unpredictable shots. It models the noise in the training data, leading it to perform poorly on unseen data.

- *Master Archer Alina's Wisdom (Bias-Variance Trade-off)*: Alina's observation about the need for balance mirrors the trade-off in machine learning. A good model strives to balance bias and variance, avoiding the pitfalls of being too rigid (high bias) or too flexible (high variance). It's about finding the sweet spot where the model is general enough to capture patterns but specific enough to predict accurately on new, unseen data.

18.3 STORY: "THE TALE OF GOLDILOCKS AND THE THREE MODELS"

ONCE upon a time in the kingdom of DataLand, a young princess named Goldilocks was tasked with predicting the number of apples that would grow in the royal orchard next year. She decided to seek help from the three famous modelers in the kingdom: Sir Bias, Lady Variance, and Lord Balanced.

Sir Bias presented his model first. He simply declared, "Every year, the orchard produces 100 apples. So, next year will be no different!" He ignored the factors like weather, soil health, or pests, stubbornly sticking to his number.

Next was *Lady Variance*. Her approach was highly detailed. She considered everything from the phases of the moon to the songs the birds were singing. However, each time she made a prediction, the number of apples varied drastically. One day she'd predict 50 apples, the next day 150, and then 75 the following day.

Figure 18.3: Prompt: A young princess in an apple orchard in digital art style

Lastly, *Lord Balanced* presented his model. He took into account significant factors like rainfall, sunlight, and past yields. His predictions were consistent and also adjusted to new information. His numbers weren't as rigid as Sir Bias nor as erratic as Lady Variance.

When the apple harvest arrived, Goldilocks found that Lord Balanced's prediction was the closest. She realized that while Sir Bias's predictions were too rigid and Lady Variance's were too erratic, Lord Balanced found the just-right middle ground.

ANALOGY EXPLANATION

- *Sir Bias (High Bias)*: His model represents a scenario with high bias where the model is oversimplified and doesn't consider all the relevant factors, leading it to consistently miss the mark. In machine learning, this is when our model makes strong assumptions and misses the underlying trend in the data.

- *Lady Variance (High Variance)*: Her constantly changing predictions symbolize high variance. A high-variance model captures too much noise and is highly sensitive to changes in the training data. In machine learning, this often leads to overfitting where the model performs well on the training data but poorly on unseen data.

- *Lord Balanced (Bias-Variance Trade-off)*: The balance that Lord Balanced achieves in his model captures the essence of the bias-variance trade-off. A good model aims for a balance between being overly simplistic (high bias) and being too complex (high variance). The optimal model generalizes well to new data while capturing the essential patterns in the training data.

18.4 EXPLANATIONS AT THREE LEVELS OF DEPTH

The following descriptions explain the "Bias and Variance Trade-off" concept in three levels of depth.

SIMPLIFIED

Imagine you're trying to throw balls into a bucket, but you're blindfolded. - **Bias** is like always missing the bucket to the left. No matter how many times you throw, you keep missing in the same direction. - **Variance** is like throwing the balls all over the place. Sometimes you miss to the left, sometimes to the right, sometimes short, sometimes long.

You want to get the right balance: not always miss the same way, but also not throw too randomly. That's the trade-off!

GENERAL

When we make predictions with a model:

- **Bias** is the error because our model is too simple. Like fitting a straight line to data that's curved. We consistently miss the mark.

- **Variance** is the error because our model is too complex. Like drawing a squiggly line that goes through every data point perfectly, but doesn't capture the general trend.

The **bias-variance trade-off** is about finding the balance. Too simple, and we miss the overall trend. Too complex, and we get lost in the noise. We want a model that's just right, capturing the main patterns without being overly swayed by the tiny details.

DETAILED

In machine learning:

- **Bias** is the error introduced by approximating a real-world problem, which may be complex, by a too-simple model. It's the difference between the expected predictions of our model and the true values.

- **Variance** refers to the model's sensitivity to small fluctuations in the training set. A high-variance model may perform well on the training set by fitting to its noise and outliers, but it generalizes poorly to new data.

The **bias-variance trade-off** represents a pivotal challenge in model selection. Models with low bias/high variance may have overfitting issues, capturing noise in the training data. On the other hand, models with high bias/low variance may be too generalized, possibly underfitting the data. The objective is to find a balance where both bias and variance are minimized, leading to a model that predicts accurately and generalizes well to new, unseen data.

Chapter 19

Overfitting & Underfitting

In our upcoming three tales, we navigate the realms of overfitting and underfitting. With each narrative's conclusion, we decode its entwined analogies. We then present lucid explanations at three levels of detail to gradually enhance the comprehension of the concept.

19.1 Story: "The Tale of Tailor Tom and the Perfect Dress"

Once in a town named Modelville, there was a famous tailor named Tom. Tom was known for his meticulous dress-making skills. One day, a lady named Lila came to him with a request to stitch a dress that she could wear on various occasions.

First Attempt (Overfitting): Tailor Tom decided to make a dress that perfectly fit every single curve and contour of Lila's body. He took precise measurements, accounting for every minute detail. The dress he made fit Lila like a glove, accentuating each and every feature. However, when Lila tried to wear the dress on different occasions, she realized the dress was too restrictive for dancing, too snug for dining, and too elaborate for casual outings. The dress was perfect only for standing still and not for anything else.

Second Attempt (Underfitting): Seeing Lila's discomfort, Tom tried again. This time, he made a very generic dress, one-size-fits-all. It was baggy, too simple, and lacked any structure. Lila found it comfortable, but it didn't look good on her. It didn't complement her figure at all. It was too basic for any event.

Third Attempt (Just Right): Tom realized his mistakes. He decided to strike a balance. He took into account Lila's specific needs and also ensured the dress was versatile. The final dress had a good fit, looked elegant, and was comfortable enough for Lila to wear on different occasions.

ANALOGY EXPLANATION

In the world of machine learning: 1. *Overfitting* is like the first dress Tom made. The model learns the training data too closely, capturing even its noise and outliers, making it perform poorly on new, unseen data. Just like the dress that was perfect for Lila standing still but not for other activities. 2. *Underfitting* is like the second dress, too generic. The model is too simple to capture the underlying patterns in the data, leading to poor performance both on the training data and new data. 3. The ideal model is like the third dress. It learns the underlying patterns without being too rigid or too loose, ensuring good performance on both training and new data.

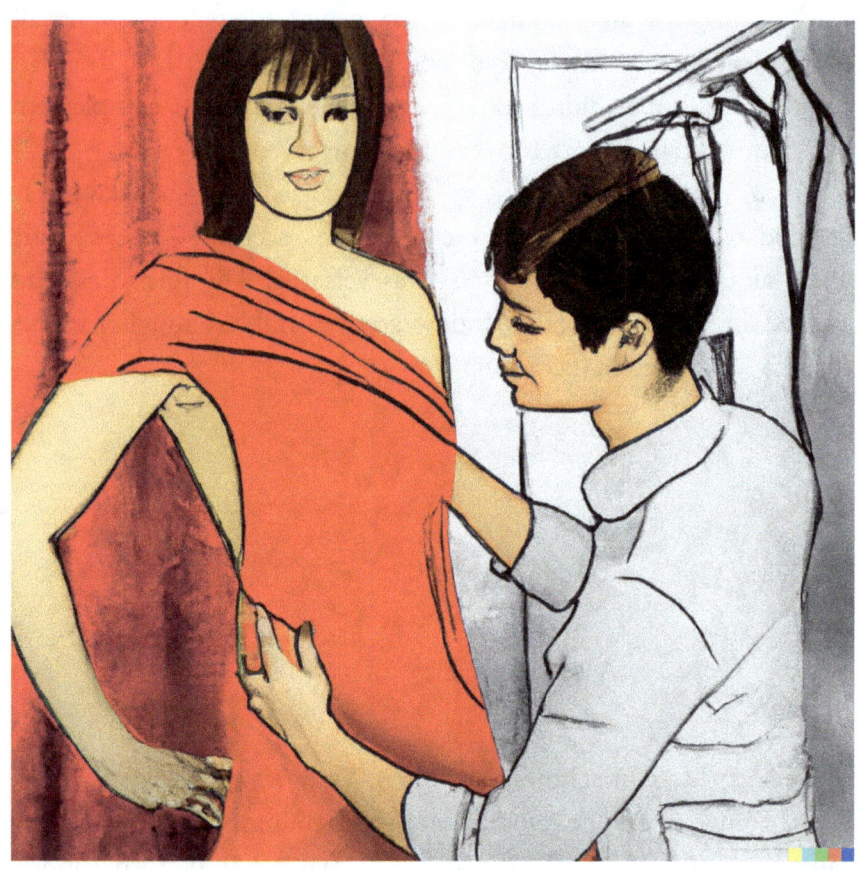

Figure 19.1: Prompt: A tailor fitting a dress on a woman in digital art style.

19.2 STORY: "THE PUZZLE OF THE GOLDEN LOCKS"

IN the heart of the Enchanted Forest, there was a treasure chest secured with three golden locks, each more intricate than the last. Two wizards, Owen and Ulysses, decided to craft keys to open these locks.

1. *Owen's Overeager Approach*: Owen was enthusiastic. He meticulously crafted a key for the first lock, detailing it with every whorl, twist, and turn of the original design. When he tried his key, it fit perfectly, but it was so finely attuned to that particular lock that it couldn't even be inserted into the other two.

For the second lock, Owen again designed a super-specific key, considering every minute detail. When it came to the third lock, he ran into an issue: some tiny changes had occurred in the lock due to wear and tear, and Owen's key, designed from the lock's original blueprint, wouldn't fit.

2. *Ulysses's Universal Design*: Ulysses took a different route. Instead of minutely crafting a key for each lock, he created one universal key, hoping it'd work for all three. His key was a generic, basic design, without accounting for the uniqueness of each lock. When he tried to open any of the locks, the key failed to turn. It was too generic for the specialized mechanisms.

Both wizards realized they needed a middle ground: a key designed with enough detail to fit the intricacies of the lock yet adaptable enough for slight variations.

ANALOGY EXPLANATION

In this story, the three golden locks represent the challenges of fitting a machine learning model to data.

1. *Overfitting (Owen's Overeager Approach)*: Owen's hyper-specific keys represent overfitting. When a model is overfitted, it performs

Figure 19.2: Prompt: A treasure chest with golden locks in a forest in digital art style.

exceptionally well on the training data, capturing even the noise or outliers (like Owen's keys with the first two locks). However, it struggles with new or slightly different data (like the third lock with wear and tear), because it has become too rigid in its understanding.

2. *Underfitting (Ulysses's Universal Design)*: Ulysses's one-size-fits-all key symbolizes underfitting. An underfitted model is too generalized and simplistic, not capturing the patterns in the data. It performs poorly on both training and new data, much like Ulysses's key that couldn't open any locks.

The best machine learning model, like the best key, should capture the essential patterns in the data without being overly rigid or overly simplistic.

19.3   Story: "The Tale of the Two Tailors"

IN the quaint town of Dataland, there were two tailors known for making outfits: Mr. Over and Mr. Under. Both were given a task to make an outfit for the mayor's annual ball.

Mr. Over, the first tailor, was known for his attention to detail. When the mayor gave him measurements, Mr. Over took them and made sure every fold, stitch, and hem matched the mayor's physique precisely. The outfit looked magnificent on the mayor, but it was so precisely tailored to him that when anyone else tried it, it didn't fit at all. In fact, it looked odd on anyone else!

Mr. Under, on the other hand, was known for making general outfits. Given the same measurements, he made an outfit that, well, resembled a bag. It fit the mayor, but it didn't look flattering. However, the loose outfit could fit many others in the town, but it didn't look particularly great on anyone.

Figure 19.3: Prompt: A tailor is fitting a dress to a woman in digital art style

ANALOGY EXPLANATION

In the story, Mr. Over represents *overfitting*. Just like the outfit he made fits the mayor perfectly but looks odd on anyone else, an overfitted machine learning model performs exceptionally well on the training data (the mayor) but fails to generalize on unseen or new data (the townsfolk).

On the other hand, Mr. Under embodies *underfitting*. His outfit fits everyone but doesn't look flattering on anyone. Similarly, an underfitted model is too generalized and doesn't perform well on either the training data or on new data.

To achieve the best results in machine learning, one must find a balance between the precision of Mr. Over and the generality of Mr. Under.

19.4 EXPLANATIONS AT THREE LEVELS OF DEPTH

The following descriptions explain "Overfitting and Underfitting" concept in various levels of complexity.

SIMPLIFIED

Imagine you have a puzzle with pieces that fit together in a specific way.

- **Overfitting**: It's like trying to cut and shape a puzzle piece so it fits perfectly in one spot, but then it won't fit anywhere else. It's too specific!

- **Underfitting**: It's when you try to make a puzzle piece fit everywhere, so you don't shape it much at all. It kind of fits everywhere, but not really well.

We want our puzzle piece (or our learning) to fit just right—not too specific and not too loose.

GENERAL

Think of training a machine to predict or learn something as training for a test.

- **Overfitting**: This is like studying only the exact questions and answers from a practice test. If the real test has the exact same questions, you'll do great. But if there are different questions, you might fail because you studied too specifically.

- **Underfitting**: This is like only reading the headings of your textbook and ignoring the details. You get a very general idea but might not do well on specific questions.

In machine learning, we want our model to learn the main patterns (or the "big ideas") without getting stuck on the tiny, unimportant details, so it does well in various situations.

DETAILED

- **Overfitting**: This occurs when a machine learning model captures not just the underlying patterns in the training data but also its noise and outliers. As a result, while the model may exhibit high accuracy on the training dataset, its performance drops significantly when exposed to new, unseen data. This is often a consequence of using an overly complex model or not employing regularization techniques.

- **Underfitting**: In this scenario, the model is too simplistic to capture the underlying patterns in the data. It doesn't perform well on the training data, and consequently, it also underperforms on new data. This might happen when the model is too simple, the features are not adequately representative, or when it hasn't been trained long enough.

The goal in machine learning is to create a model that generalizes well to new data, which means striking the right balance between capturing patterns (without getting swayed by noise) and maintaining a certain level of simplicity.

Chapter 20

Regularization

The upcoming trio of tales illuminates the concept of "Regularization in Machine Learning." After each story, we'll unravel the thoughtful analogies woven into the narrative. Following these, we present clear and concise explanations of the concept at three levels of complexity, helping readers enhance their understanding step by step.

20.1 Story: "Capturing the Essence"

In a quaint village, there was a famous painter named Elara. She was renowned for capturing the essence of the village in her paintings. One day, the village children challenged her to paint a scene by adding every single detail they pointed out, from every leaf on a tree to every brick in a house. Elara took on the challenge and started painting. As she added more and more details, the painting became chaotic and confusing. The essence and beauty of the village were lost amidst the myriad of details.

Seeing the cluttered canvas, an old sage named Lenn advised her, "Elara, sometimes to truly capture the essence, you need to leave

Figure 20.1: Prompt: A young woman painting a complex picture of a town scene in digital art style.

out some details. Let the strokes be simple and fluid." Heeding his advice, Elara started another painting, this time focusing on the main features of the village and using broader strokes. The end result was a masterpiece, capturing the village's spirit, even without every tiny detail.

ANALOGY EXPLANATION

In the world of machine learning, the process of training a model is like painting a picture. Without regularization (like Elara's first painting), the model tries to fit every single data point (or detail), leading to a phenomenon called overfitting. This makes the model perform well on the training data but poorly on new, unseen data.

Regularization (the advice from sage Lenn) is a technique used to prevent overfitting. By adding a penalty for complexity (like using broader strokes and leaving out minute details), the model is guided to be simpler and focus on the main patterns in the data. This results in a model (or painting) that captures the essential patterns and performs well on both the training data and new, unseen data.

20.2   STORY: "SALLY'S LEMONADE STAND"

Once upon a time in the small town of Regville, a young girl named Sally decided to set up a lemonade stand in her front yard. To attract more customers, she decided to put up a sign displaying the temperatures at which lemonade sales were highest.

Every day, she noted down the temperature and the number of lemonades she sold. Sally, being a perfectionist, wanted her sign to be extremely accurate. She drew a graph with temperatures on one axis and lemonade sales on the other.

At first, Sally tried to draw a line that passed through every single point on her graph. She wanted complete accuracy – a perfect match between temperature and sales. However, the line she drew was jagged and full of sharp turns; it looked like a mountain range, twisting and turning to touch every data point.

Her wise older brother, Sam, noticed her struggle and suggested a simpler approach. "Your sign is too complicated," he said. "People just want to know if they should buy lemonade when it's hot or cold, not at every specific temperature. Let's simplify it."

Figure 20.2: Prompt: A young girl selling lemonade in her front yard in digital art style.

Taking Sam's advice, Sally adjusted her line to be smoother and more straightforward, even though it didn't pass through every data point exactly. The new line showed a clear general trend: sales went up as it got hotter.

The next day, customers flocked to Sally's stand as the temperature rose. They appreciated the clear and simple message of her sign, which made sense and was easy to understand.

ANALOGY EXPLANATION

In this story, Sally's initial attempt to draw a line through every single data point on her graph represents a machine learning model that is overfitting. Just like Sally's complex and jagged line, an overfitted model is overly sensitive to the noise and fluctuations in the training data; it is trying to capture every detail of the data, including the random noise.

When Sally's brother, Sam, advises her to simplify the line, he is introducing the concept of regularization. Regularization in machine learning is akin to simplifying that line on the graph. It imposes a penalty on overly complex models, encouraging the algorithm to prioritize simplicity and general trends over fitting the noisy or random fluctuations in the training data.

In our story, the simpler, more stable line that Sally ends up using is akin to a regularized machine learning model. It captures the underlying trend in the data (that lemonade sales increase as it gets hotter) without being overly sensitive to small fluctuations in temperature on any given day – it generalizes well. This is the essence of regularization: it helps us to build models that are simpler, more interpretable, and better at making predictions on new, unseen data.

20.3 STORY: "THE ARTIST AND THE SCULPTOR"

ONCE upon a time in a small coastal village, there lived an artist named Alina and a sculptor named Samuel. They were great friends and loved to create art, but their approaches were different.

Alina was a painter who aimed to capture every detail in her surroundings. She would paint the leaves on trees with intense detail, down to the smallest vein. However, her paintings were often so packed with details that people found it hard to see the overall scene. The trees, the sky, and the people in her paintings were lost in a sea of intricate details.

Samuel, on the other hand, was a master of marble sculptures. He knew that removing too much stone could ruin a piece, so he always aimed for simplicity. One day, he gave Alina some advice: "Think of your painting as a block of marble," he said. "Start with the big, broad strokes to outline the scene, and then add just enough detail to bring it to life, but not so much that you lose the essence of what you're trying to portray."

Taking this advice to heart, Alina began to approach her paintings differently. She focused on the essential elements that captured the spirit of the scene, avoiding excessive detail that could overwhelm the viewer. Her paintings transformed, becoming clearer and more beautiful, and people could now see and appreciate the stories she was telling through her art.

ANALOGY EXPLANATION

In this story, Alina's initial painting approach is analogous to a machine learning model that overfits the data. Her intense focus on capturing every tiny detail in her paintings is like a model that learns the noise in the training data, fitting it too closely. In such cases, the model becomes complex and fails to generalize well to new, unseen data, just like how Alina's overly detailed paintings made it hard for people to see the overall scene.

Samuel, the sculptor, represents the concept of regularization in machine learning. His advice to Alina—to focus on the essential elements and avoid excessive details—is akin to adding a penalty term to the loss function in a machine learning model. This penalty discourages overly complex models (those with large coefficients/weights), pushing the model to be simpler and smoother, much like Samuel's elegant and simple sculptures. It allows the model to learn the important patterns in the data

Figure 20.3: Prompt: A young sculptor working on a marble sculpture in digital art style

while avoiding the trap of overfitting to the noise, thus enabling better generalization to new data.

The marble block in Samuel's advice symbolizes the raw data, and the act of sculpting (or painting with restraint, in Alina's case) parallels the process of training a model with regularization—a process of carefully uncovering the underlying structure in the data without overcomplicating the final result.

20.4 EXPLANATIONS AT THREE LEVELS OF DEPTH

The following descriptions explain the "Regularization" concept at three levels of depth.

SIMPLIFIED

Imagine you are trying to draw a line with your ruler through a bunch of stickers on a paper, and you want the line to be as close as possible to all the stickers. But, if you try to make the line wiggle and twist to touch every single sticker, it might look like a squiggly mess!

Regularization is like a friend who gently holds your hand steady, so the line you draw is nice and smooth, without all the squiggles. This way, even if your line doesn't touch every sticker, it still looks neat and does a pretty good job.

GENERAL

Think of fitting a curve (like a line) through a scatter plot of data points in your math class. Without regularization, the curve might become very wiggly and complex, trying to pass through every data point – this is overfitting. Overfitting is like memorizing the answers to a test – it doesn't mean you understand the material.

Regularization is a technique that helps to simplify that curve, making it smoother and less wiggly. It's like a penalty for making the curve too complicated; it encourages the curve to be as simple as possible while still doing a good job of explaining the trend in the data.*

DETAILED

Regularization is a fundamental concept in machine learning that addresses the problem of overfitting, where a model learns the training data too well and generalizes poorly to new, unseen data. This is achieved by adding a penalty term to the loss function that the model is trying to minimize. There are different forms of regularization, such as L_1 (Lasso), which adds the sum of absolute values of the weights, and L_2 (Ridge), which adds the sum of squares of the weights to the loss function. The strength of the regularization is controlled by a hyperparameter, often denoted as λ(lambda). By increasing λ, you increase the penalty, and thus constrain the model's complexity, steering it towards simpler, more generalizable solutions. Regularization effectively introduces bias into the model, reducing its variance and helping to mitigate the tradeoff between bias and variance, as articulated in the Bias-Variance Decomposition.*

CHAPTER 21

HYPERPARAMETER TUNING VIA GRID SEARCH, RANDOM SEARCH, AND BAYESIAN SEARCH

In the forthcoming trio of narratives, we embark on the journey of "Hyperparameter Tuning via Grid Search, Random Search, and Bayesian Search". Upon concluding each story, we demystify its incorporated analogies. Following this, we provide lucid explanations, structured at three levels of detail to help readers to gradually enhance their comprehension.

21.1 STORY: "THE GREAT COOKIE BAKE-OFF"

IN the town of Modelville, there was an annual competition called the Great Cookie Bake-off. Everyone in town was eager to bake the most delicious cookie. Sarah, a young baker, decided to participate this year, and she had a recipe for chocolate chip cookies but wasn't sure about the right amounts of some ingredients.

1. *The Grandmother's Notebook (Grid Search)*: Sarah remembered her grandmother's old notebook, which listed various combinations of ingredients for the perfect cookie. It specified different amounts of sugar, chocolate chips, and butter. Sarah decided to bake batches of cookies using every single combination listed in that notebook, ensuring she didn't miss any possible winning recipe.

2. *The Whimsical Cousin's Method (Random Search)*: Sarah's cousin, Tim, also wanted to participate. Instead of using any notebook, he thought it would be fun to randomly decide on the amounts of sugar, chocolate chips, and butter for each batch. He believed in luck and hoped that one of his random combinations would hit the jackpot.

3. *The Chef Neighbor's Wisdom (Bayesian Search)*: Sarah's next-door neighbor, Chef Ray, took a different approach. He baked one batch of cookies and tasted them. Based on that taste, he'd guess which ingredient was a bit too much or too little. He continuously improved his recipe based on his previous results, making intelligent tweaks every time.

Results Day: Sarah, Tim, and Chef Ray all presented their best cookies. While Sarah's systematic approach and Tim's randomness resulted in some delicious cookies, it was Chef Ray who took the prize. His iterative, thoughtful adjustments led him to the perfect balance of ingredients.

ANALOGY EXPLANATION

- *Grandmother's Notebook (Grid Search)*: Just like Sarah tried every combination from the notebook, grid search tries every hyperparameter combination to find the best one. It's systematic but can be time-consuming.

Figure 21.1: Prompt: A young woman baker cooking chocolate chip cookies in digital art style.

- *Whimsical Cousin's Method (Random Search)*: Like Tim, who relied on randomness, random search tries random combinations of hyperparameters. It can sometimes find good results faster than a grid search but might miss the best combination.

- *Chef Neighbor's Wisdom (Bayesian Search)*: Bayesian search, similar to Chef Ray's approach, builds on previous results to intelligently choose the next set of hyperparameters to test. This can lead to finding better combinations faster than the other two methods.

21.2   STORY: "THE GOLDEN LOCK QUEST"

IN the mystical land of Algorithma, there was a legendary golden lock said to protect immense treasures. To unlock it, one had to adjust three dials to the perfect settings. The trio of brave adventurers – Gideon Grid, Ronny Random, and Beatrice Bayesian – set out on individual quests to unlock the golden lock and claim the treasure.

1. *Gideon Grid's Thorough Approach*: Gideon believed in patience and precision. He meticulously started from the very beginning, turning each dial one notch at a time, testing every single possible combination. It was a methodical process. He believed that by trying every possibility, he would certainly find the correct setting.

2. *Ronny Random's Lucky Strategy*: Ronny thought the world was built on chance and serendipity. Instead of going step by step, he spun the dials randomly, hoping luck would be on his side and he'd stumble upon the right combination.

3. *Beatrice Bayesian's Informed Guesses*: Beatrice adopted a different strategy. She'd heard tales from old adventurers about similar locks. Using that knowledge, she made an educated guess and tried a combination. Depending on how close it felt, she'd

Figure 21.2: Prompt: A grand door secured with a large golden combination lock in digital art style.

adjust her next guess, using previous information to get closer and closer to the perfect settings.

End of the Quest:

While all three adventurers had their methods, Beatrice, with her iterative and informed strategy, unlocked the golden lock faster than the others, claiming the treasures of Algorithma.

ANALOGY EXPLANATION

- *Gideon Grid's Thorough Approach (Grid Search)*: Grid search, like Gideon, tries every possible combination of hyperparameters systematically to find the best setting. While it ensures no combination is missed, it can be exhaustive and time-consuming.

- *Ronny Random's Lucky Strategy (Random Search)*: Much like Ronny's reliance on luck, random search randomly selects hyperparameter combinations. It might hit the right combination sooner than grid search but without the guarantee of systematic coverage.

- *Beatrice Bayesian's Informed Guesses (Bayesian Search)*: Bayesian optimization, represented by Beatrice, utilizes information from the past to make better future decisions. By constantly refining based on previous outcomes, it aims to reach the optimal setting efficiently.

21.3 STORY: "THE QUEST FOR THE PERFECT POTION"

IN the mystical town of Algora, there was a yearly challenge to create a magical potion with the perfect balance of ingredients to shine the brightest. Three young wizards – Gideon, Rael, and Luna – set forth to craft this potent brew.

1. *Gideon's Ancient Scrolls (Grid Search)*: Gideon possessed an ancient set of scrolls inherited from his ancestors. Each scroll detailed precise quantities of dragon tears, fairy dust, and moonbeams. Knowing the value of thoroughness, Gideon meticulously brewed a potion for every combination prescribed by these scrolls, ensuring he tested all possible blends.

2. *Rael's Dice of Destiny (Random Search)*: Rael, a free spirit, possessed the Dice of Destiny. Each side of these dice had a different ingredient quantity inscribed. Every day, Rael would

roll the dice to determine the mixture for his next potion. He believed in serendipity and hoped that fate would guide him to the luminous concoction.

3. *Luna's Reflecting Pool (Bayesian Search)*: Luna had a magical reflecting pool that shimmered with insights. After concocting a potion, she'd gaze into the pool, which hinted at what needed to be adjusted for a brighter shine. Each potion Luna made was informed by the feedback from the previous ones, steadily improving her brew's luminosity.

Grand Reveal: On the day of the challenge, each wizard showcased their most radiant potion. While Gideon's structured approach and Rael's trust in randomness produced gleaming vials, it was Luna, with her iterative wisdom, who unveiled the most dazzling potion.

ANALOGY EXPLANATION

- *Gideon's Ancient Scrolls (Grid Search)*: Similar to Gideon's methodical approach, grid search exhaustively experiments with every hyperparameter combination provided. It leaves no stone unturned but can be resource-intensive.

- *Rael's Dice of Destiny (Random Search)*: Just as Rael relied on the whims of his dice, random search tests random hyperparameter combinations. It may stumble upon a great result early on but doesn't guarantee the best outcome.

- *Luna's Reflecting Pool (Bayesian Search)*: Like Luna's adaptive method, Bayesian search refines its hyperparameter choices based on past performances. It builds on feedback to more efficiently hone in on an optimal solution.

Figure 21.3: Prompt: A magical potion with the perfect balance of ingredients to shine the brightest in digital art style.

21.4   EXPLANATIONS AT THREE LEVELS OF DEPTH

The following descriptions explain "hyperparameter tuning concept and grid search, random search, and bayesian search" at increasing levels of complexity.

SIMPLIFIED

Imagine you're trying to make the perfect cup of hot chocolate. You can change how much cocoa, sugar, and milk you add. These are like the "settings" or "dials" for your hot chocolate. Now, to find the yummiest cup:

- **Grid Search** is like trying every combination of cocoa, sugar, and milk, one by one.

- **Random Search** is like randomly mixing different amounts and tasting to see which one's best.

- **Bayesian Search** is smarter. After each taste, it thinks about what might be better and tries that next.

Hyperparameter Tuning is just like adjusting the settings to get the best hot chocolate!

GENERAL

When we train a machine learning model, there are certain settings, or "dials", we can adjust called hyperparameters. Tuning these can help our model perform better.

- **Grid Search**: This is systematically checking every combination of hyperparameters. Think of it like checking every cell in a table to find the best one.

- **Random Search**: Instead of checking everything, we randomly pick some combinations to try out. It can be quicker than grid search but might miss the best combo.

- **Bayesian Search**: This is a smarter way. After trying a combination, it makes a guess about which settings might be better based on what it has learned so far.

Hyperparameter Tuning is the process of adjusting these settings to get the best performance from our model.

DETAILED

In machine learning, models come with **hyperparameters**, which are external configurations that aren't updated during model training. Their optimal values are crucial for model performance.

- **Grid Search**: It's an exhaustive search method. Given a list of hyperparameters, it evaluates the model performance for every possible combination. It's computationally expensive and might not be feasible for a large hyperparameter space.

- **Random Search**: As opposed to evaluating all combinations, random search samples a fixed number of hyperparameter combinations from a distribution for each hyperparameter. While less systematic, it can be more efficient and yield better results than grid search in less time.

- **Bayesian Search**: This approach builds a probability model for the objective function and uses it to select the most promising hyperparameters to evaluate in the true objective function. It's based on the Bayesian optimization framework and can often find better hyperparameters faster than the previous methods.

Hyperparameter Tuning is the overarching process of optimizing these configurations to improve model validation performance, and different strategies, like the ones mentioned, offer various trade-offs in terms of computational cost and efficacy.

CHAPTER 22

ENSEMBLE LEARNING

In the upcoming set of stories, we traverse the realm of Ensemble Learning. After each chronicle, we clarify its interlaced analogies. Next, we present crisp explanations, designed to engage readers by presenting the concept at three levels of complexity, helping readers gradually enhance their grasp.

22.1 STORY: "THE SYMPHONY OF EXPERTS"

IN the bustling town of Predictville, there was an annual competition called "The Ultimate Predictor." The town's residents would come forth with their own methods of predicting whether it would rain on the last day of the year.

One year, three unique contestants caught the attention of Predictville.

1. *Anna, the Historian*: Anna would look at all the past years when it rained and tried to find patterns. She had a massive collection of journals detailing every single day.

2. *Bob, the Birdwatcher*: Bob believed that birds acted differently when it was about to rain. He would sit for hours noting down the behavior of birds and making predictions based on it.

3. *Charlie, the Cloudwatcher*: Charlie had an affinity for clouds. He believed that certain cloud formations were indicative of rain.

Separately, each of them had their strengths and weaknesses. Anna sometimes missed out on new patterns not in her journals, Bob's method was slightly unreliable if birds migrated, and Charlie could get confused with similar-looking cloud formations.

On the day of the competition, a young girl named Daisy had an idea. Instead of relying on one predictor, why not consult all three? She proposed a committee – an ensemble of these experts. Each expert would make a prediction, and the majority would win.

When the day came, Anna predicted it would rain, Bob said it wouldn't, but he wasn't too confident, and Charlie was sure it would rain based on the clouds. Daisy took the majority vote: Rain it was! And, as predicted by the ensemble, it did rain, winning them the competition.

ANALOGY EXPLANATION

In this story, each expert (Anna, Bob, Charlie) represents an individual model in ensemble learning. While they are good on their own, they might have individual shortcomings. By combining their expertise, we can often get a better and more reliable prediction, just like ensemble methods in machine learning. The process of consulting all three and going with the majority vote mirrors the technique of ensemble learning, where multiple models' predictions are combined to get a final result.

Figure 22.1: Prompt: A group of experts making a careful judgment in digital art style.

22.2 STORY: "THE SYMPHONY OF MODELS"

Once upon a time in the kingdom of Dataville, a grand competition was announced. The king wished for a melody that would represent the heart and soul of his kingdom, and thus, musicians from all over were invited to play their best piece. Each musician represented a different machine learning model, with their unique strengths and weaknesses.

Among the competitors, there was Ada, a flutist, whose notes were soft and gentle, but sometimes lacked depth. Then there was Forest, a cellist, with deep and resonant notes, yet occasionally he would miss the tempo. Gradient, a violinist, played rapid, soaring sequences, but could sometimes be off-pitch. And then many other musicians, each with their unique touch.

The competition began, and one by one, each musician played their melody. Some were breathtaking, some were decent, and some faltered. It was clear that none of them were perfect on their own.

A wise old conductor named Ensemble had been observing quietly. As the individual performances concluded, he made a proposition. "Instead of competing," he suggested, "why not join forces and play together, covering each other's weaknesses and highlighting each other's strengths?"

The musicians hesitated but decided to give it a try. Under the guidance of Ensemble, they started playing together. Ada's flute filled the gaps in Forest's cello notes, and Gradient's violin added the missing energy and pace.

The resulting melody was harmonious, robust, and resonant. It was neither the flute, cello, nor the violin, but the combination of all, playing at their best, creating a sound none thought was possible.

Figure 22.2: Prompt: A symphony playing music together in digital art style.

The king was overjoyed and declared that the melody produced by the group would be the new anthem of Dataville.

ANALOGY EXPLANATION

- Each musician represents a machine learning model with its strengths and weaknesses.
  - The conductor, Ensemble, symbolizes the ensemble learning technique.

- The combined melody signifies the improved accuracy and robustness achieved by combining the predictions from various models.

- Just as the combined orchestra produced a more harmonious and complete melody than any individual instrument, ensemble methods in machine learning leverage the strengths of individual models to create a more accurate and robust combined model.

22.3   STORY: "COMBINING WISDOMS"

IN a small town named Modelville, the town council had a tough decision to make about the annual town festival's location. To ensure that the best decision was made, the council invited several wise people from neighboring towns to help decide. Each of these wise people had their own unique way of thinking, and their experiences varied widely.

1. *Mr. Bagging*, who came from the Forest Town, believed in asking multiple friends (trees) for their opinions and then making a decision based on the majority. When he wasn't sure, he would just take an average of their views.

2. *Ms. Boosting*, from the Dynamic Dale, would ask one friend for advice, and based on what went wrong with that advice, she would adjust and ask the next friend. She would keep adjusting until she felt she had the best solution.

3. *Sir Stacking* from the Layered Lagoon believed in a layered approach. He would ask several of his wise friends for advice, and then have his most trusted advisor make a final decision based on all their inputs.

4. The council also knew about *Captain Voting* from Democracy Dunes, who always believed in letting everyone have a say and then picking the most popular choice.

After listening to all, the council realized the strength in combining these techniques. Instead of relying on a single method,

Figure 22.3: Prompt: A council of people making a decision in a town hall in digital art style.

they incorporated wisdom from all the methods, ensuring the best possible outcome for the town festival.

ANALOGY EXPLANATION

- *Modelville* represents a dataset that needs a prediction or classification.
  - *Wise people* represent different algorithms or models.
  - *Mr. Bagging's approach* symbolizes *Bagging* in ensemble learning, where multiple versions of a model are created, and

their outcomes are averaged (for regression) or voted upon (for classification).

- *Ms. Boosting's strategy* stands for *Boosting*, where models are built sequentially, with each new model correcting the errors of the previous ones.

- *Sir Stacking's technique* denotes *Stacking*, where predictions of multiple models are used as inputs in a new model to make final predictions.

- *Captain Voting* exemplifies the *Voting* method, where predictions from different models are combined based on majority voting or averaging predicted probabilities.

22.4   EXPLANATIONS AT THREE LEVELS OF DEPTH

The following descriptions explain the "Ensemble Learning" concept at different levels of complexity.

SIMPLIFIED

Imagine you're trying to guess the number of candies in a jar. Instead of just making one guess yourself, you ask several friends for their guesses. Then, you combine everyone's guesses to come up with a better, more informed guess. This is like ensemble learning: combining many guesses to make a better final guess.

GENERAL

In ensemble learning, instead of using just one method or algorithm to make a prediction, we use multiple ones and then combine their predictions. Think of it like a group project: each member of the group contributes their part, and in the end, you combine everyone's work for the final presentation. There are different ways to combine these predictions. For instance:

- **Bagging:** Create multiple versions of the same model and then average out their predictions.

- **Boosting:** Build models one by one, where each new model tries to correct the mistakes of the previous one.

- **Stacking:** Use the predictions of several models as inputs to another model that makes the final prediction.

The idea is that by combining multiple models, we can often get more accurate and stable predictions than using just one model alone.

DETAILED

Ensemble learning is a paradigm in machine learning where multiple models, often referred to as "weak learners," are trained to solve the same problem and are then combined to get better results. The primary reason for using ensemble methods is to reduce overfitting, increase robustness, and improve predictive performance. Key techniques in ensemble learning include:

- **Bagging (Bootstrap Aggregating):** This method involves creating multiple subsets of the original dataset using sampling with replacement. An individual model is trained on each subset. Predictions are aggregated through voting (for classification) or averaging (for regression). An example is the Random Forest algorithm.

- **Boosting:** Here, models are trained sequentially. Each subsequent model focuses more on the instances that were wrongly predicted by its predecessor. Predictions are often weighted and combined. Popular algorithms include AdaBoost, Gradient Boosting Machine, and XGBoost.

- **Stacking:** Multiple models are trained, and their predictions are used as features for another "meta-model" that tries to learn the best way to combine these predictions.

The central premise of ensemble methods is that when weak learners are combined, they can produce a more powerful "strong learner" that performs better than any individual model.

CHAPTER 23

ENSEMBLE LEARNING METHODS (BAGGING, BOOSTING, AND STACKING)

In the ensuing collection of tales, we navigate the intricacies of Ensemble Learning Methods, encompassing Bagging, Boosting, and Stacking. After each saga, we decode the enfolded analogies. What follows are lucid explanations, fashioned to resonate with readers by providing the same concept at three levels of detail to incrementally enhance the understanding.

23.1 STORY: "THE KINGDOM'S SEARCH FOR THE PERFECT FRUIT SALAD"

IN a kingdom far away, the king announced a contest to find the best fruit salad recipe for the royal feast. Chefs from all over the land were invited to present their creations. The three top chefs, Baron Bagging, Duchess Boosting, and Sir Stacking, each had their unique approach.

1. *Baron Bagging's Brigade*: Baron Bagging believed in the power of many. He asked 100 chefs from his brigade to create a salad each. Every chef was given a random set of fruits; some fruits may appear more than once across different sets, and some might be missing. After everyone prepared their salads, Baron took a bit from each and combined them into one massive bowl, ensuring the taste was diverse and balanced.

2. *Duchess Boosting's Technique*: Duchess Boosting took a step-by-step approach. She first let her apprentice make a salad. Tasting it, she noticed the missing elements or overrepresented fruits. In the next round, she emphasized getting those proportions right. With each subsequent attempt, the salad got better, focusing more on the parts that were previously neglected.

3. *Sir Stacking's Symphony*: Sir Stacking had a unique approach. He invited three chefs, each known for their signature fruit salads. Once each chef presented their dish, Sir Stacking didn't just want to combine them. Instead, he let his master taster taste each salad and then decide the right proportion of each to mix for the ultimate fruit salad.

At the feast, the king was so impressed that he couldn't choose a winner. He realized that diversity in approaches, like in the fruit salads, is what makes the kingdom rich and thriving.

ANALOGY EXPLANATION

- Just like Baron Bagging's approach of combining multiple salads (models) to get a diverse and balanced flavor, bagging in ensemble learning involves creating multiple models on random subsets of the data and then averaging the results (in regression) or voting (in classification) to get the final prediction.

Figure 23.1: Prompt: A delicious fruit salad in digital art style.

- Duchess Boosting's approach of iteratively refining the salad resembles boosting in machine learning. Models are trained sequentially, with each one focusing on the mistakes of its predecessor, resulting in an improved combined prediction.

- Sir Stacking's method of blending the best parts of each chef's salad mirrors stacking in machine learning. Different models (salads) are trained, and their predictions are then used as inputs to another model (the master taster), which determines the best combination for the final output.

23.2 STORY: "THE ORCHESTRA STORY OF ENSEMBLE LEARNING"

IN a small town named Ensembville, the mayor decided to host a grand music concert. The idea was to produce the most harmonious and delightful music the town had ever heard.

1. *Bagging (The Independent Bands)*: The mayor invited several local bands to play their version of a famous song independently. Each band had a slightly different set of instruments and members. After all bands had performed, their music was merged, taking the best parts from each band's rendition, creating a beautiful and balanced melody.

2. *Boosting (The Continuous Improvement Band)*: There was one band in the town that had a unique approach. They started by performing the song once. After the performance, they identified their mistakes or the parts that lacked harmony. In their next performance, they particularly focused on those weak areas while still playing the entire song. They repeated this process, improving each time. Eventually, their rendition was a version where all their past mistakes had been iteratively improved upon.

3. *Stacking (The Grand Finale)*: For the final act, the mayor had a brilliant idea. He invited representatives from each band to form

Figure 23.2: Prompt: A grand music concert in the town square in digital art style.

a supergroup. Each member played the part of the song they were best at. But there was a twist! The mayor brought in a famous conductor from a neighboring city to guide this supergroup. The conductor listened to each player's strength and coordinated them, leading to an unparalleled symphonic masterpiece.

ANALOGY EXPLANATION

1. *Bagging*: Each band playing independently and then merging their best parts is similar to training multiple models on different

subsets of data and then aggregating their outputs. Just as each band had variations in their instruments and members, each model sees a slightly different subset of data. The aggregation, whether through majority voting or averaging, is akin to taking the best parts from each rendition.

2. *Boosting*: The Continuous Improvement Band's iterative approach mirrors the process of boosting. In boosting, algorithms learn from the mistakes of the preceding ones. Each subsequent model attempts to correct the errors made by the previous models, just as the band tried to iteratively improve upon their prior performances.

3. *Stacking*: The supergroup with the conductor embodies the idea of stacking. Different models (or band members) bring their individual strengths (or best parts of the song). The conductor, acting as the meta-model, harmoniously blends these strengths to achieve a superior performance, similar to how stacking uses a higher-level model to optimally combine the predictions of base models.

23.3   Story: "The Art of Cooking the Perfect Dish"

IN a quaint village, there was an annual cooking competition. Every chef aspired to create the perfect dish. Three chefs - Benny, Betsy, and Stanley - had distinct methods of refining their dishes over the years. Their techniques became legendary and were known as Bagging, Boosting, and Stacking.

Benny's Bagging Method: Benny believed in the power of collaboration. Every year, he'd invite multiple chefs to cook their version of the same dish. While each chef had a slightly different style and ingredient mix, they were all working from the same core recipe. After they finished, Benny would combine the best parts of each dish to create a single, superior version. This method allowed Benny to capture the strengths of each individual chef's approach.

Betsy's Boosting Method: Betsy was a perfectionist. Each year, she'd prepare her dish and then invite a panel of judges to critique it. Instead of getting disheartened by the criticism, she'd use the feedback to her advantage. If her sauce was too salty, she'd adjust it; if her veggies were undercooked, she'd focus on improving that. With each iteration, Betsy's dish got progressively better, honing in on perfection by learning from past mistakes.

Stanley's Stacking Method: Stanley admired both Benny and Betsy and believed that their methods had merit. So, he combined them. He'd first use Benny's collaborative approach and invite chefs to cook their versions of the dish. Once that was done, he'd take the best elements from each dish and make a combined version. But Stanley didn't stop there. He then asked Betsy to taste this combined dish and give her expert feedback, refining it even further. This two-step refinement process led to a dish that was often unparalleled in taste and quality.

ANALOGY EXPLANATION

- *Bagging (Benny's Method)*: Just as Benny invited multiple chefs to cook their versions of a dish and then combined the best parts, bagging involves training multiple models on different subsets of data and aggregating their results to get a final prediction. It reduces variance and provides a more stable result.

- *Boosting (Betsy's Method)*: Betsy's iterative approach to perfecting her dish mirrors the boosting technique, where algorithms train models sequentially, focusing on improving where they previously made mistakes. The idea is to continually enhance the model's performance.

- *Stacking (Stanley's Method)*: Stanley's method of combining the strengths of both Benny and Betsy mirrors stacking. In stacking, predictions of several base models are used as input for another

Figure 23.3: Prompt: An annual cooking competition in a village in digital art style.

model (meta-model) to make a final prediction, harnessing the strengths of each base model.

23.4 EXPLANATIONS AT THREE LEVELS OF DEPTH

The following descriptions explain "Ensemble Learning Methods, Bagging, Boosting, Stacking" at various levels of detail.

SIMPLIFIED

Imagine you're trying to solve a jigsaw puzzle.

- **Bagging**: You invite several friends over, and you each try to solve the puzzle on your own using different sections of the pieces. Later, you all come together and combine your sections to get the final picture.

- **Boosting**: Imagine you and your friends trying to solve the puzzle together, but you focus more on the parts that you found difficult in your previous attempt. This way, each time you're trying, you're getting better at the tricky parts.

- **Stacking**: Now, imagine you first ask a few friends to solve the puzzle. After they give their best attempts, you then ask your best puzzle-solving friend to fix any mistakes and combine their solutions to make the best picture.

GENERAL

- **Bagging**: Bagging is like taking multiple quizzes on the same topic. For each quiz, you get a subset of all possible questions, and you might take the quiz multiple times with different questions each time. In the end, you average your scores from all the quizzes to get your final score. This is how algorithms like Random Forest work.

- **Boosting**: Here, you take the quiz multiple times, but each time you focus more on the questions you got wrong the last time. Over time, you improve on your weak points, and your overall score gets better. Algorithms like AdaBoost or Gradient Boosting work this way.

- **Stacking**: For stacking, imagine you're taking a final exam. But instead of relying on just one study method, you first use flashcards, then group study, and maybe online tutorials. You take notes on each method's insights and combine them for the best understanding. Similarly, in stacking, you combine the strengths of multiple machine learning algorithms using another algorithm on top.

Detailed

- **Bagging (Bootstrap Aggregating)**: This method involves generating multiple subsets (or samples) from the training dataset using bootstrap sampling. Then, an individual model is trained on each of these samples. The final predictions are obtained by aggregating the predictions of all models, usually through majority voting for classification problems or averaging for regression. The Random Forest algorithm is a classic example of bagging, where decision trees are used as the base learners.

- **Boosting**: Boosting algorithms train models sequentially. Each subsequent model is built by focusing on the instances that were wrongly predicted by the previous models. This is achieved by assigning higher weights to misclassified instances. The final prediction is a weighted sum or a weighted vote of all the individual model's predictions. AdaBoost, Gradient Boosting Machine (GBM), and XGBoost are examples of boosting algorithms.

- **Stacking**: In stacking, multiple base models are trained on the dataset, and their predictions are used as input features for a meta-model (or a higher-level model). The meta-model learns the optimal combination of the base models' predictions to achieve a better performance. This method leverages the strengths of different models and offsets their individual weaknesses.

CHAPTER 24

REINFORCEMENT
LEARNING

In the forthcoming series of tales, we journey through the captivating world of Reinforcement Learning. As each story unfolds, we decipher its woven analogies. This is followed by crystalline explanations, designed to enlighten readers with three levels of detail, helping them enhance their understanding step by step.

24.1   STORY: "THE GREAT MAZE OF LEARNOVIA"

In the enchanted realm of Learnovia, there was a vast, ever-changing maze called Labyrinthus. Within its twisting turns and mysterious pathways lay a prized golden token. Many had entered, but few found their way to the treasure.

Enter Theo, a young adventurer. Unlike others who entered with maps or listened to tales of those who attempted before, Theo had a magical wristband – a gift from a wise sorceress.

Every time Theo took a step in the right direction, the wristband gave a warm, encouraging buzz. If he took a step in the wrong direction, it remained cool. And if Theo made the same mistake multiple times, the wristband would give a gentle pinch, ensuring he remembered not to repeat it.

At first, Theo wandered aimlessly, relying on the wristband's subtle signals. But with time, he began to recognize patterns and started predicting which paths would earn him the warm buzz. Some routes led to pleasant surprises, like a sip of water or a clue, which made Theo even more determined to find the token.

It wasn't long before Theo, guided by the feedback from his wristband, navigated through Labyrinthus, finding the golden token.

When he emerged, triumphant, the spectators were in awe. "How did you find your way so swiftly?" they inquired. Theo held up his wristband, remarking, "It's not about knowing the right path, but learning from every step."

ANALOGY EXPLANATION

- *Labyrinthus*: Represents the complex environment where an agent (like Theo) must operate in reinforcement learning.

- *Theo's Adventure*: Theo's journey within the maze symbolizes the trial-and-error nature of reinforcement learning, where an agent takes actions without knowing the outcome but learns from the consequences.

- *Magical Wristband*: The wristband embodies the reward (or feedback) mechanism in reinforcement learning. Positive feedback (warm buzz) is akin to a reward, the cool feel signifies neither reward nor punishment, and the pinch is like a negative reward or penalty. Over time, by seeking the positive feedback and avoiding the negative, Theo (the agent) learns an optimal strategy to navigate the maze (environment).

Figure 24.1: Prompt: A mysterious great maze in digital art style.

24.2 STORY: "THE ADVENTURE OF ROBBY THE ROBOT IN VIDEO GAME LAND"

IN the digital realm of Video Game Land, there was a curious little robot named Robby. Robby wasn't like the other characters in the game who followed a strict script. Instead, he was free to roam and play various games within this land.

One day, Robby stumbled upon an arcade hall titled "Master the Game." Intrigued, he entered to find a single game console with multiple levels. There was no instruction manual, only a scoreboard displaying points.

With a shrug, Robby started playing. At first, he didn't understand the rules. Sometimes he'd touch a green gem, and a "ding" sound would occur, adding points to his score. But whenever he bumped into a red spike, a loud "buzzer" sounded, and he'd lose points.

Initially, Robby was hesitant. But as he played more, he started to recognize patterns. Green gems were good; red spikes were bad. He also realized that some paths gave more points than others, and soon he was strategizing, trying to maximize his score.

Every once in a while, the game would introduce new elements—a blue portal that would teleport him or a gold coin that gave a huge point boost. Though these additions made the game more challenging, Robby's experiences helped him decide whether to approach or avoid them.

After countless hours, Robby became the top player in "Master the Game," not because he had an instruction manual but because he learned from every move he made, continually improving his strategy.

Figure 24.2: Prompt: A robot playing video games in digital art style.

ANALOGY EXPLANATION

- *Video Game Land*: Represents the environment in which reinforcement learning operates.
- *Robby the Robot*: Symbolizes the agent in reinforcement learning that interacts with the environment.
- *Master the Game Arcade*: Represents the specific task or challenge that the agent needs to learn.
- *Scoreboard*: Reflects the reward system in reinforcement learning. Just as Robby earns points for favorable actions and loses them for mistakes, reinforcement learning agents receive positive rewards for good decisions and penalties for bad ones.
- *No instruction manual*: Reinforcement learning doesn't have explicit instructions on how to achieve a task but learns optimal strategies through interaction and feedback.
- *Green gems and red spikes*: Analogous to positive and negative rewards in reinforcement learning, guiding the agent to learn beneficial actions.
- *New game elements (blue portal, gold coin)*: Represent the dynamic nature of many environments where the agent must adapt to new situations and challenges.
- *Learning from every move*: Reinforces the concept of trial and error in reinforcement learning, where agents learn the best strategies by experiencing consequences and adapting their actions accordingly.

24.3 STORY: "LUNA AND THE MAGIC ARCADE"

IN the quaint town of Pixelville, Luna, a young girl with a keen sense of adventure, stumbled upon a hidden arcade named "FuturePlay." Inside, there was a game she had never seen before – "Quest for the Starlit Crown."

This game was unlike any other. There were no set levels, no instructions, and no patterns to memorize. Every time Luna inserted a coin, the game started in a new, unpredictable world. The goal was clear: find the Starlit Crown. But how to get there was a mystery.

At first, Luna faced many challenges. She'd move her character right and fall into a pit, losing a life. Then she'd try going left and be rewarded with a glowing gem. Every decision she made had a consequence – sometimes good, sometimes bad. But Luna was undeterred. Each gem she collected gave her points, and each monster or pit she avoided kept her in the game longer.

With each play, Luna began to realize something magical. The game was teaching her! When she made smart decisions, she earned more points and progressed further. When she made poor choices, she'd quickly lose. But every loss was a lesson.

Over time, Luna became an expert. She realized it wasn't about memorizing paths but understanding how her actions affected the outcome. Some days she'd prioritize collecting as many gems as possible. Other times, she'd focus on avoiding dangers, all while keeping her eye on the ultimate prize: the Starlit Crown.

One day, after months of play, Luna finally obtained the Starlit Crown, amidst a burst of digital fireworks and triumphant music. The other kids in Pixelville were in awe. "How did you master such an unpredictable game?" they asked. Luna smiled and replied, "I let the game teach me."

ANALOGY EXPLANATION

- *FuturePlay Arcade*: Represents the unknown environment in which reinforcement learning operates.

- *Quest for the Starlit Crown*: Symbolizes the reinforcement learning process, where there's a clear goal but no set instructions on how to achieve it.

Figure 24.3: Prompt: A young girl playing games in an arcade in digital art style.

- *Luna*: Represents the agent in reinforcement learning, learning through interaction, trial, and error.
- *Glowing Gems*: Analogous to the rewards in reinforcement learning, guiding the agent toward beneficial actions.
- *Pits and Monsters*: Represent the challenges or penalties in the environment which deter the agent from certain actions.
- *Earning Points*: This signifies the reward mechanism in reinforcement learning, where the agent receives feedback based on its actions.
- *Obtaining the Starlit Crown*: Demonstrates the culmination of learning, where the agent has successfully learned an optimal strategy from its environment.

24.4   EXPLANATIONS AT THREE LEVELS OF DEPTH

The following descriptions explain "Reinforcement Learning" at increasing levels of complexity.

SIMPLIFIED

Imagine you're playing a video game where you're a character exploring a magical world. You don't have a map or instructions. Every time you make a move – like jumping over a pit or collecting a coin – the game gives you points or takes them away. If you jump into the pit, you lose points. If you collect a coin, you gain points. Your goal is to figure out how to earn the most points and reach the end of the game. Just like in this game, reinforcement learning is when a computer learns by trying different actions and seeing which ones give the best results!

GENERAL

Reinforcement learning (RL) is a type of machine learning where an agent learns by interacting with an environment. It's like playing a game: the agent takes actions (like moves in a game), the environment responds (you might get points or lose a life), and then the agent gets a reward or penalty based on the outcome. The agent's goal is to figure out the best strategy or set of actions that will get it the most rewards over time. Think of it as training a pet: when it does something good, it gets a treat (positive reward), and when it does something wrong, it might get a timeout (negative reward or penalty). Over time, the pet learns the best behaviors to get treats.

DETAILED

Reinforcement learning (RL) is an area of machine learning where an agent learns by interacting with its environment to maximize some notion of cumulative reward. The agent makes sequential decisions by observing the current state of the environment, taking an action, receiving a reward, and transitioning to a new state. The objective is to learn a policy – a mapping from states to actions – that maximizes the expected sum of future rewards. The learning process is guided by the exploration-exploitation trade-off: the agent must decide whether to try out new actions (explore) or stick to the actions it believes to be optimal based on past experiences (exploit). Algorithms like Q-learning, Deep Q Networks (DQNs), and Policy Gradient Methods are common techniques used to solve RL problems, adapting and optimizing the agent's policy as it learns from its interactions.

CHAPTER 25

REINFORCEMENT LEARNING TERMINOLOGIES (AGENT, ENVIRONMENT, STATE, ACTION, REWARD, AND POLICY)

In the upcoming collection of narratives, we traverse the intricate landscape of Reinforcement Learning Terminology, touching on elements like Agent, Environment, State, Action, Reward, and Policy. With each tale's conclusion, we demystify its embedded analogies. What follows are lucid explanations, sculpted to engage readers by presenting the subject at three levels of detail to gradually enhance the comprehension of the concepts.

25.1 STORY: "THE TREASURE HUNTER"

IN a mysterious land, there was a young treasure hunter named Alex. Alex's sole aim was to find the legendary golden goblet hidden deep within a vast, unpredictable jungle. Every morning, Alex would stand at a specific spot in the jungle, look around, and decide which direction to take to hopefully find the goblet.

The jungle was dense and ever-changing. Sometimes Alex would find a trail, other times a river, a cave, or even wild animals. Depending on what Alex encountered (the current situation in the jungle), he would decide on an action: to move forward, turn back, use a tool, or set up camp.

Whenever Alex made good decisions, like finding a safe spot to rest or discovering a clue to the goblet's location, he would find little silver coins as a sign of being on the right track. However, wrong decisions, like encountering a wild animal or getting lost, resulted in losing some of these coins. The ultimate reward, of course, would be finding the golden goblet.

Over time, Alex started noting down his decisions in a journal, detailing what he saw and what action he took. As days passed, this journal served as a guide, helping him make better decisions based on previous experiences.

ANALOGY EXPLANATION

1. *Agent*: Alex represents the agent. He makes decisions and takes actions based on his current situation and past experiences to achieve his goal.

2. *Environment*: The vast, unpredictable jungle is the environment. It's what the agent interacts with and where it receives feedback based on its actions.

Figure 25.1: Prompt: A young treasure hunter in a jungle in digital art style.

3. *State*: Each situation Alex encounters, like finding a trail, river, or wild animal, represents a state of the environment.

4. *Action*: The decisions Alex makes in response to each situation, like moving forward, turning back, or using a tool, represent actions.

5. *Reward*: The silver coins Alex finds (or loses) after each action serve as rewards (or penalties). They indicate how good (or bad) the decision was concerning the ultimate goal of finding the golden goblet.

6. *Policy*: Alex's journal, which helps him decide what action to take based on his current situation and past experiences, is akin to a policy. It's a strategy or set of rules that guides the agent's decisions in each state.

In this way, the story offers a relatable visualization of reinforcement learning terminology, making it easier to understand and remember.

25.2   STORY: "THE ADVENTURE OF LITTLE TOMMY IN CANDYLAND"

ONce upon a time in the colorful world of Candyland, there was a curious boy named Tommy. Tommy loved candies, and he had just one goal every day: to collect as many candies as he could!

1. *Agent*: Tommy is our adventurer or agent. He's the one making decisions and exploring Candyland.

2. *Environment*: Candyland itself, with its winding paths, candy trees, and gumdrop mountains, is the environment. It's the world where Tommy moves and from which he collects candies.

3. *State*: At any given moment, Tommy might be standing by the lollipop trees, or next to the chocolate river, or on top of the

gumdrop mountain. Each of these locations is a different state in which Tommy finds himself.

4. Action: From each spot or state in Candyland, Tommy can choose what to do next. He might decide to climb a mountain, cross a bridge, or dive into the river to find underwater candies. These decisions are his actions.

5. Reward: Now, not all candies are created equal. Some are just sweet, while others have a surprise center! Every time Tommy takes an action, like diving into the chocolate river, he might get a regular candy or a super special candy with a surprise. The type and number of candies he gets are his reward. Some actions might even lead to sour candies, which he doesn't like!

6. Policy: Tommy starts to notice patterns. By the lollipop trees, it's usually best to look under the leaves. In the mountains, the candies are often hidden behind rocks. These strategies or sets of actions Tommy takes in different parts of Candyland form his policy for candy collection. It's his game plan for getting the most and best candies every day.

ANALOGY EXPLANATION

- *Agent (Tommy)*: In reinforcement learning, the agent is like Tommy, making decisions and trying to achieve a goal.

- *Environment (Candyland)*: The environment is the world where the agent operates. It's everything outside the agent and responds to the agent's actions.

- *State (Locations in Candyland)*: The state represents the current situation or context the agent is in.

- *Action (Decisions Tommy makes)*: Actions are the decisions the agent can make in each state.

- *Reward (Type of candy)*: Rewards are feedback from the environment based on the agent's actions. It tells the agent how good the decision was.

Figure 25.2: Prompt: A boy picking candies in a magical room full of candies in digital art style.

- *Policy (Tommy's candy collecting strategy)*: A policy is a strategy or set of rules the agent follows to decide what action to take in each state.

Through this adventure, Tommy learns the best ways to navigate Candyland, just as an RL agent learns to navigate its environment to maximize rewards!

25.3   STORY: "THE KNIGHT'S QUEST FOR THE GOLDEN APPLE"

In a vast, mystical kingdom, there was a brave knight named Sir Aiden. Sir Aiden had a unique mission: to find the legendary Golden Apple that was believed to bestow great knowledge upon its possessor.

1. *Agent (Sir Aiden, the Knight)*: Sir Aiden, with his armor and sword, represents the decision-maker or the learner. He's the one actively making decisions based on his experiences and knowledge.

2. *Environment (The mystical kingdom)*: This entire kingdom, filled with dense forests, treacherous mountains, and hidden caves, is the world where Sir Aiden operates. It gives feedback to Sir Aiden's actions and influences his journey.

3. *State (Current situation)*: At one moment, Sir Aiden might find himself standing at the edge of a cliff, and the next moment, he might be inside a dragon's lair. Each of these scenarios or places represents a unique state or situation Sir Aiden is in.

4. *Action (Decisions)*: In every state, Sir Aiden makes decisions. At the cliff's edge, he might choose to turn back. In front of the dragon, he might decide to either fight or flee. These decisions are the actions he takes in response to each state.

5. *Reward (Outcome of actions)*: For every action, there's a consequence. If he decides to fight the dragon and wins, he might find a map pointing towards the Golden Apple - a positive reward.

Figure 25.3: Prompt: A mystical knight on his horse with a golden apple in his hand in digital art style.

But, if he loses, he might end up injured, which would be a negative reward. These outcomes, whether good or bad, guide Sir Aiden's future decisions.

6. *Policy (Strategy)*: Over time, Sir Aiden develops a strategy or a set way of making decisions. If he knows that friendly elves live in the forests, he might choose to always visit forests to get help, believing that it's the best action to take whenever he's near one.

ANALOGY EXPLANATION

- *Agent*: Just as Sir Aiden is the main character making decisions, in reinforcement learning, the agent is the entity that learns from its actions and the feedback it gets.

- *Environment*: The mystical kingdom is the environment that responds to the agent's actions. Similarly, in RL, the environment gives feedback on the agent's actions.

- *State*: The situations Sir Aiden finds himself in are analogous to states in RL, which represent the current scenario or context.

- *Action*: Sir Aiden's decisions parallel the actions in RL which are the choices made by the agent.

- *Reward*: Just as Sir Aiden receives outcomes (good or bad) for his actions, the agent in RL receives rewards (positive or negative) for its actions.

- *Policy*: Sir Aiden's strategy of decision-making is similar to the policy in RL, which is a strategy that the agent adopts over time to maximize its rewards.

25.4 EXPLANATIONS AT THREE LEVELS OF DEPTH

The following descriptions explain "Reinforcement Learning terminology: Agent, Environment, State, Action, Reward, Policy" in three levels of detail.

SIMPLIFIED

Imagine you're teaching a pet robot!

- **Agent**: Think of the robot as the "learner" or the "player". This is like you when you play a video game.

- **Environment**: This is where the robot is and where it plays, like a game board or a playground.

- **State**: It's like a spot on the game board. Depending on where the robot is, it will see different things and have different options.
- **Action**: What the robot decides to do, like move forward, turn left, or grab something.
- **Reward**: If the robot does something good, it gets points or treats. If it does something not-so-good, it might lose points.
- **Policy**: This is like a rulebook the robot makes for itself. If it notices it gets more points by doing a certain thing in a certain place, it'll remember that and do it again!

General

Consider a video game analogy.
- **Agent**: This is the character you control in a video game.
- **Environment**: The game world. It's everything your character interacts with and includes all the challenges and tasks.
- **State**: The current situation or scene in the game. For example, your character's health, location, and items it has.
- **Action**: What you decide to make your character do, like jump, attack, or use an item.
- **Reward**: Points you earn or lose in the game based on how well you play. Beat a boss? Earn points. Fall into a trap? Lose points.
- **Policy**: It's like a strategy guide that your character develops from playing. It helps decide the best action to take based on past experiences to earn the most points.

Detailed

Dive into the world of iterative algorithmic learning.
- **Agent**: An autonomous entity that observes and acts upon an environment to achieve some goal. It's the decision-making unit that learns from the consequences of its actions.

- **Environment**: The external context or system with which the agent interacts. It provides feedback to the agent based on the agent's actions.

- **State**: A configuration or representation of the environment at any given time. It's a point in the state space, which could be finite or infinite, discrete or continuous.

- **Action**: Any choice or decision made by the agent that affects the state. It's selected based on a certain policy to maximize future rewards.

- **Reward**: A scalar feedback signal indicating the success of an action in a given state. The agent's objective is to maximize the cumulative reward over time.

- **Policy**: A strategy that the agent employs to determine the next action based on the current state. It's a mapping from states to actions that's either deterministic or stochastic and is refined over time to optimize long-term rewards.

ABOUT THE EDITOR

Dr. Oguzhan Topsakal is a multifaceted professional with expertise spanning research, teaching, design, and development. He earned his B.S. in Computer Engineering from Istanbul Technical University, followed by M.S. and Ph.D. degrees in Computer Science from the University of Florida.

With a rich background in the software industry, Dr. Topsakal now serves as an Assistant Professor in the Department of Computer Science at Florida Polytechnic University. He instructs a range of courses, encompassing machine learning, deep learning, algorithm design, databases, and mobile development. Dr. Topsakal is passionate about pioneering new approaches and solutions through machine learning and deep learning.

Thanks & Contact

Thank you for reading this book. I genuinely hope that its unique storytelling approach and three levels of explanations of the concepts helped you grasp machine learning in a memorable and engaging way.

Your thoughts and suggestions are highly valued, and I warmly welcome your feedback. Please feel free to reach out to me if you have a new concept you'd like to see included in future editions, or if you notice an error that needs correcting. Your insights and contributions are greatly appreciated.

If you encounter any stories in the book that appear misleading or inaccurate, I encourage you to reach out with a concise explanation of your concerns. Your input is vital in continually refining and enhancing the content of this book.

Contact Email: topsakal.books@gmail.com

Sincerely,

Florida, August 2023

Oguzhan Topsakal, Ph.D.